ANDRÉ MALRAUX

Saturn
An Essay on
Goya

Translated by
C. W. Chilton

GOYA: *Portrait of Marquesa de las Mercedes*. Paris, Louvre

SATURN
AN ESSAY ON
GOYA

BY ANDRÉ MALRAUX

PHAIDON PUBLISHERS INC

DISTRIBUTED BY GARDEN CITY BOOKS

NEW YORK

THE ORIGINAL EDITION WAS PUBLISHED

BY GALLIMARD · PARIS

IN LA GALERIE DE LA PLÉIADE

UNDER THE TITLE :

SATURNE · ESSAI SUR GOYA

TRANSLATED FROM THE FRENCH

BY

C · W · CHILTON

© PHAIDON PRESS LTD 1957

5 CROMWELL PLACE · LONDON SW7

MADE IN GREAT BRITAIN

PRINTED BY HUNT, BARNARD & CO LTD

AT THE SIGN OF THE DOLPHIN · AYLESBURY · BUCKS

PREFACE

ALTHOUGH *this book does not form part of the* Psychology of
Art *I have given it the same form because the plates in it perform
the same task. They scarcely belong to what historical studies
call illustration; they do not accompany the description of works
but replace it and, like the shots in a film, are intended on occasion to
convey a suggestion by their content or by the order in which they occur.*

Just as in the Psychology of Art *I assumed a knowledge of the broad
outlines of the history of art, so here I assume the life and work of Goya
to be known. Many pictures familiar to everyone have been left out. My
object is not that of the biography, nor that of the 'comprehensive study';
these are excellent but do not represent finality.*

*This essay sets out to answer the questions asked in the short preface to
my edition of the* Goya Drawings, *to which the reader is referred.
Almost all the works that will be shown, after the* Preliminaries,
remained more or less secret. The sale of the Caprichos *was stopped;
neither the* Disasters *nor the* Disparates *were put on sale in Goya's life-
time; the paintings in the* House of the Deaf Man *were known only to
a small number of persons. These vehement sermons were hardly preached
at all and Goya, like Pascal, was famous for his talent but a genius
only to posterity. His genius lies not only in having broken with the
demand for harmony and having taken horror for his province, it lies in
having discovered a style the equal of the great religious styles. It is this
that I have endeavoured to analyse here.*

A.M.

VICENTE LÓPEZ: *Portrait of Goya at the age of eighty*. Madrid, Prado

6

GOYA: *Self-Portrait at the Age of about 65*. Vienna, Kunsthistorisches Museum

PRELIMINARIES

NO genius seems more spontaneous than his. His dreams, his reality, his style, even that break in the pencil-line by which his workmanship can be recognized at the first glance – all were his own creation. And then we reflect that it took forty years for him to become Goya.

And yet, like all young painters of his time he worked first in the Italian style; carefully and with gusto. The element of fluidity in his early drawing is not at all foreign to baroque drawing; there is the same hostility to outline, the same preference for marked contrasts of light and shade. But they are not the same contrasts.

He must have seen in Rome the canvases of Magnasco, who was still famous, and in them no doubt met with picaresque settings, the taste for the gypsy, the ape, and the plumage of the cock, and with the torments in the landscapes of Piranesi – the world of Italian comedy set down by a hand, superior to that of Callot, which began with freaks and ended with the Inquisition. Magnasco before him had realized what death gains from the masquerade and had surmised the effect produced by the Inquisition's ridiculous cap above a tortured face. But his genius inclined towards setting; passing from the masque to torture through the stages of the quack and the barber he accompanied them all with strains from the Venetian Carnival and so successfully made poetry of them that he lifted them above drama. Confronted with

MAGNASCO: *Scene of the Inquisition.* Vienna, Kunsthistorisches Museum

Italy, the language of mightier Spain is always the same; in the Rome where El Greco had regretted that Michelangelo did not know how to paint, where Velazquez had said of Raphael nothing but 'I don't like that at all', we can imagine Goya standing before an Inquisition of Magnasco or his school and thinking, 'How good it would be, if it were true . . .'

The idea of truth, in painting, is, to say the least of it, indistinct. Nothing of Magnasco entered into the canvases of Goya on his return from Italy. He asserts that he followed only three masters; nature, Velazquez, and Rembrandt. By nature did he mean truth? He cared very little for the other kind; we have to ransack his etchings to find a tree. His world is made up of men and stones. There is often an arch dominating everything, a shadow suggesting bridge or porch, or more often a hiding place; occasionally there is a distant crag, site of some legend of the under-world, or those arid vistas of Arab towns with their Catholic belfries revealed in the light of Judgement Day in the *Third of May, 1808*. Without painting ruins he evoked ghosts of towns; no one else has achieved that. Against this background of stone (arch, wall, prison) everything belongs to man. The 'nature' he speaks of is himself. A 'true' Inquisition would have been a scene which was not concerned only with its setting, and a torment that had a real meaning.

MAGNASCO: *Soldiers' Concert*. Paris, Private Collection

If Goya had died at the age of thirty-five how could we say that he had been pre-destined to destroy the art of decoration, the art that aimed to give pleasure? He would have been a baroque painter among others, a portrait painter, occasionally rising above the common level, and the designer of tapestry cartoons of disturbing pungency whose vast superiority to those of Francisco Bayeu would be less apparent if we were not seeking in them the first murmurings of a voice which later became peremptory. What genius does not come to the help of its earlier efforts? We cannot look at the drawing of a mantilla without thinking of it. These cartoons are charming; their charm increases, from the earliest to those executed for the Duke of Osuña's *Alameda*. This is all too obvious. To recognize the central theme of the *Count of Orgaz* in the Grecos of Venice, and of *Lost Illusions* in *Jane the Pale* ultimately becomes ridiculous; all the more so in this case as the small number of genre pictures left by the Goya of the early style is an invitation to count these cartoons among works that are masterpieces, and to compare the *Sunshade* with the *Majas Out Walking* of Lille. These tapestries, however are nothing but tapestries, and obedient to the laws of what was then a decorative art; this Goya is more like Bayeu than the Goya of the House of the Deaf Man. In a fashion brilliant but quite purposeless, if we remember that he was to become a master of world painting, he turns into something Spanish the world of Venice and of the *Fêtes Galantes*. Here are ill-shaven guitar players, bulls with their tails in the air, Figaros who under their three-cornered hats fling their arms wide in theatrical gestures. Tapestry demands pure

tints, the seductive reds of the *China Merchant*; and he shows both an energy that bewitches us (we have forgotten his Spanish rivals and contemporaries) without surpassing that of the *Singeries* of Chantilly nor counting for much when placed beside Fragonard or Watteau, and at the same time an uneasy intensification of his theatrical world, a rejection of charm for the leaden colour scale of the *Injured Mason*. We should not presume to equate him with Guardi – he will be Goya.

Like Bayeu, he complied in his cartoons (just as he made his portraits stand out from their background) with the light haze of the fresco – the haze against which stand out ruins and masts – that Turner was later to glorify. His realism at that time consisted in this, that while he idealized them by means of somewhat awkward elegance, he painted real people against non-existent backgrounds. Their blurred shadows set them in motion. But let this art once

GOYA: *Blind Man's Buff*. Madrid, Prado

try to escape from its tapestry stage-setting, let footlights and backcloth disappear at one and the same time, and its minor character becomes quite evident. Only once did Goya attempt what many Gothic painters before him had tried to do in the details of their landscapes – to balance by the richness of the substance of his clear tints the dark patches standing out from them. This is in the *Meadow of San Isidro*, an inverted triangle formed by dark masses of people between the two parts of a foreground of light-coloured clay. The subject was fashionable but Goya treats it with a richness and an emphasis which were quite new. He gives his lights the weight of shadows by the richness of a coloration which derives from that of over-loaded Velazquez canvases, from make-up, and from lacquer. He is no longer painting a cartoon but a picture. And the pre-eminence of this specific treatment which he put in place of a representation rejects that element which, in his previous cartoons and canvases, had belonged to the 'objective vision', the element which had subordinated the picture painted to the subject represented, or to the wish to charm. It is hard

13

GOYA: *The Meadow of San Isidro*. Madrid, Prado

GOYA: *Fight before an Inn.* Madrid, Prado

to imagine the accents of Manet in a picture of Raphael. Previously, the ever-changing freedom of his touch (which it is quite wrong to call impressionist) had belonged entirely to tapestry. But now he wanted to paint pictures instead of spectacles or theatrical settings. Such a change could not take place without inter-mediate stages. Even though the Meadow is a rough draft which owes nothing to the colours of Venice, it owes a great deal to its spirit. There had been Magnasco, his predecessors and his imitators; there had been Guardi; there had also been Hals, whom he seems not to have known very well – and whose art he might perhaps have overlooked, because there was still Velazquez.

Velazquez he knew well. No one had been more susceptible to the kingly pleasure of painting, to the annexation of the transitory world of the Great by the invincible might of the picture. But the art which only escapes from a hidebound discretion through the casual presence of genius remained in harmony with the world he depicted. He did not put himself in its place. The hair of his blond infantas were his strokes but were also locks that could be caressed; their clothes were his strokes but they were also of satin; he glorified his dismal Spain with his colour as Raphael had glorified his triumphant Rome with his drawing. But glorification was not Goya's purpose; in the interval between Velazquez ceasing to paint and his own beginning, a fundamental word had dropped out of circulation – majesty.

The whole of Europe had put charm in its place. But painting, with Guardi as with Fragonard, as with the English school, still struggled with the weapons of a

16

WATTEAU: *La Finette*. Paris, Louvre

WATTEAU: *The Country Meeting*. Dresden, Gallery

former age against the threat of illustration; and a cartoon is not a picture. What words can express the difference between painting and taste – between Guardi and Bayeu, between *La Finette, The Embarkment for Cythera, The Country Meeting*, or the *Lesson of Love* of Watteau and *The Vintage* or even the *Soldier and the Girl*, one of Goya's better cartoons; between *Indifference* and *The Sunshade*? The Spanish picturesque was not peculiar to Goya, it did not express him yet. It had been fore-shadowed by Viladomat, is discernible in Camaron, Carnicero, Manuel de la Cruz, Paret and Castillo; in the Bayeus and many others. The *Pelele* (which cannot even be reproduced beside the canvas of a master) holds the attention principally because it is bound up with the whole of the Goya-to-be; to put it on an equal footing with a great *tableau* of the same age or the same spirit, with Guardi, Fragonard, Hogarth, or Watteau – or with the other admirable *Pelele* of the *Disparates* – is almost ridiculous, and this aspect of Goya's art had no such ambitions. There are in his cartoons sensitive combinations of colours and even, in the *Mason* and many others,

19

Goya: *Picnic*. London, National Gallery

20

GOYA: *Winter*. Madrid, Prado

new combinations. But painting is not just a palette. All great artists of taste know how ephemeral that is and try to explore it until they can apportion to it its share of immortality. To realize how fragile the art of his cartoons is, Goya only had to compare it with that of the *Meadow*. No doubt he himself regarded it as a minor art, although he had great difficulty in freeing himself from it, except in his portraits.

In them he set out to paint. There is a certain amount of garishness in many of them but this aims less and less at pleasing. Their charm, a little English at first, is on occasion discarded to reveal the highest poetry; their colouring sometimes gives place to the brilliant austerity of Spain. The reds of the *Soria Child* and of the little *Manuel Osorio* have no longer any connection with taste. There only in all Goya's work until he was forty-five does his genius show through. For the rest, what is there? Religious art which is nothing of the kind, dazzling frescoes devoted to national, rustic, and elegant compositions – the age itself summed up.

1792. Illness was about to sweep away these dreams just as the Revolution a little later would sweep away their models. Goya recovered but was disabled; he believed, according to his friends, that he had brought it on himself. Deaf now, he was afraid of going blind. His case grew hopeless. One of the charming artists of the eighteenth century was expiring.

GOYA: *Mirrors I.* Drawing. Madrid, Prado

GOYA: *Portrait of Don Manuel Osorio de Zuñiga*. New York, Metropolitan Museum

CAPRICHOS?

TO allow his genius to become apparent to himself it was necessary that he should dare to *give up aiming to please*. Cut off from everyone by deafness he discovered the vulnerability of the spectator, he realized that the painter has only to struggle with himself and he will become, sooner or later, the conqueror of all. His solitude, he says, 'makes room for observation'. Of what? For the Academy of San Fernando he painted the *Burial of the Sardine*, the *Madhouse*, the *Flagellants*, 'to occupy his mind, mortified by the contemplation of his troubles' and solely, he believes, 'from a desire to record the testimony of truth'.

He would have been no less concerned with truth had he painted a woman walking along the street. That which is called the realism of Goya is not so much the result of observation as everyone, himself included, maintains, as it is conferred by the fantastic. The accent of the 'popular scenes' in his tapestries grips us more than that of Italian scenes does because it is more austere (Spain is Spain) and because we add to it the accent of his future genius. But these scenes, like almost everything at that time called popular, have little to do with the people and much to do with theatricals. And if suddenly he produces a striking painting of an old woman's face the order in which his pictures were produced suggests that he found the accent not by studying his models but by making etchings of witches. At forty-five he had engraved little, and most of his work had been reproductions of pictures. There can be no doubt that he had been impelled towards the art of etching by loneliness. He engraved to please himself, even as he was to paint the figures of the House of the Deaf Man; he did not publish either the *Disasters of War* or the *Disparates*. From the beginning of his illness his engraved work became in quality and in extent comparable with his painted work.

He began with the twenty-four *Caprichos*. But what is a *Capricho*? Is it the illustration of a caption? Most of the captions have been added to the drawings. Sometimes they are ejaculations, or even comments. 'Bravo! – Who would have believed it! – Look, how grave they are! – A prosperous journey!' under the etchings, and 'She has the look of an honest woman. – Little it concerns us!' under the drawings, clearly arising out of the sketch and not giving it a name. And the frequent 'this': 'These people believe in birds. – This girl knows it well. – This one has plenty of parents' shows Goya's astonishment before figures which are partly strangers to him. How then can we regard him as an illustrator? It is he that would be illustrated by literature. He draws as one in a dream and asserted, in the *Visions of a Night*, that he drew his dreams. But night is not as rational as this; let him but describe his nightmares in detail and we see that he had come to dream his drawings. This

GOYA: *Young Man Fighting*. Drawing. Valencia, Academy of San Carlos

GOYA: *Two Angels*. Fresco. Madrid, S. Antonio de Florida

27

obsessed genius was obsessed by his own creations and these too orderly dreams are more like drawings than his drawings are like dreams . . .

Besides, he went on to add commentaries to his figures after he had engraved their captions. Under flight of demons in *A Prosperous Journey* he wrote, 'Where is this hellish company going, filling the air with its cries?' He classified them, 'These,' he noted under the plate of the *Goblins*, 'are another kind; jolly, amusing, obliging, perhaps a little greedy and inclined to play tricks; but still, kindly little fellows.' 'If you had not come at all,' he writes with less irony beneath another, 'it would not have mattered very much.' Some remarks are more intriguing, 'It is a remarkable thing that this kind will not allow itself to be seen except at night and in the dark. No-one has found out where they lock themselves up and hide in the day-time. But if anyone were to be fortunate enough to uncover a nest of goblins, lay hold of it and show it in a cage, etc.' In no way does he speak as though he had control of them. By 'fantasies' he means particularly things that cannot be foreseen. He does not so much premeditate these images as accept them; images less of dreams than of dreaming. For ages men had banished them.

In those days albums often had as their justification a common subject; views of a town, the unfolding of a Biblical episode, for instance; even those of Piranesi are collections of imaginary views. What does Goya owe to the *Capricci* of Tiepolo? Hardly what the *Madhouse* owes to his tapestries . . .

Although he forebore 'to ridicule particular shortcomings in this or that individual', his art was so disconcerting, and the public so given to passing judgement on an artist instead of following him, that for fifty years the *Caprichos* were regarded as pictures of manners intermingled with freakish imaginings. It was long before it was noticed that they consisted of two books, one following the other: the first, containing plates 1 to 43, includes almost all the so-called scenes from social life; the second, which begins with '*The Sleep of Reason brings forth Monsters*' includes, in nine-tenths of the plates, witches, demons, and goblins. Clearly this division was intended by Goya, for the '*Sleep of Reason*' is a frontispiece, and seems to have been one from the first. It is the only plate where an inscription is found as early as the second preparatory sketch, '*Ydioma universal, dibujado y grabado por F. de Goya*', which was to be turned into a famous heading. Again, it is in the first part of the album, where Goya has engraved subjects apparently least involved with the fanciful – love affairs, intrigues, femininities – that his treatment is least inclined to caricature. As the fantastic nature of the scene grows more obvious, so the irony is emphasized. Why do we forget that he had been blind to it for twenty years? It appears – and it is strange indeed – that he discovered irony at the same time as spectres, and so as to make fun of them rather than of his contemporaries. But every satirical drawing assumes what it satirizes, and thereby suggests it.

The style of his religious work had been conventional; that of his cartoons is

GOYA: *Mirrors II*. Drawing. Madrid, Prado

29

GOYA: *The Sleep of Reason*. Preparatory drawing. Madrid, Prado

often too polished, and sometimes dazzling with a brilliance which emulates that of the *Singeries*. The style of the drawings in the first *Caprichos*, or of those executed not long before them, is one of broken lines, always seeking to capture a mantilla, embroidery, ribbons – the style we find in many pages of the albums of San Lucar and later, not without a certain rather facile humour, in the woman with the scythe and the serpent. But Goya had already found another in which his genius was beginning to show itself and which was something more than a style – that of the rapidly executed workmanship for the *Garter*, the pencil version of which was

Buen Viage.

GOYA: *Prosperous Journey*. Etching. (Capricho 64)

GOYA: '*God forgive her — it is her mother.*' Drawing. Madrid, Prado

GOYA: *Woman Fainting*. Drawing in the Album de San Lucar. Madrid, Prado

still faltering. Even as though it had been born of agony it shows itself in the *Man in the Iron Collar* (from the *Mirrors*), angular and quite different from that of the individual with the pointed shoes whom he transmogrifies. This is the style which was to reach its full powers of simplification in the plate of the *Female Prisoner* in the *Caprichos*. Goya would retain it all his life; prodigiously enriched, it would re-appear in *The Last Communion of St. Joseph of Calasanz* and in *The Agony in the Garden* – at a time when his workmanship might have begun to show hesita-

33

Goya: *The Garter*. Drawing. Madrid, Prado

34

tion. But already, even in the stylistically least developed *Caprichos*, the flowered ornamentation has disappeared. The black mantilla in *It was her Mother*, which has become a head of hair, is no longer stressed, neither is the white headdress; the lines of the lace have lost their wish to charm, and the fan no longer has the edging whose accent matched that of the eyes. The renunciation of allurement did not, it is true, give Goya his new style but it allowed him to develop it. An entire race of new figures, the representation of which is *a representation in two dimensions*, was in process of multiplying before his eyes; there were caricatures.

This multiplication was, first and foremost, a *new fact*. Before comparing the style of the journalists of the nineteenth century with that of their counterparts of the eighteenth it is wise to remember how important was the birth of journalism, without which neither Balzac nor Dickens would have been quite the writers we know; in the same way, caricature, which for generations had been a game, became a world of its own, a confused world (like that of journalism) into which entered comedy, satire, the lampoon, and a freedom that painting had not known to the same degree. Its two spheres of activity were politics and manners; and among the latter, fashions. This meant that, like journalism, it was hostile to the traditions of art because its principal subject-matter was inseparable from current events, and that the caricaturist, seeking only to produce an intensified expression of a passing scene, thought little of the durability of his work. Lastly, caricature was familiar with a field of minor importance but wide extent, the field of rustic subjects. In the eighteenth century the peasant world had been an exotic one in which the aristocracy of the Court and the city artisans had embodied their dreams; to the middle classes it was becoming a ridiculous world which allowed them to assert their superiority, a world of the past and the picturesque, a 'costume world' as opposed to the world of the future. The noble savage was becoming simply a savage. Goya turned aside from all that; *he* knew the countryfolk. But all caricature was a creation of a new world of the imagination. The kinship which unites the pages of many of the *Caprichos* with contemporary burlesques is not, it must be added, a close family relationship. Ushered in by Hogarth, caricature was destined to spread over the entire nineteenth century and one of the geniuses of that century, Daumier, would be a caricaturist. It is possible without difficulty to establish the existence of an English influence on French work, followed by a whole collection of inter-acting influences; but it is fruitless to ask what plates of any particular great English caricaturists impressed themselves on Goya's mind. Although he adapted some of them it was not their style which appealed to him but the very existence of caricature, the existence of a world which by virtue of its nature escapes from the 'laws of art'. An artist does not live only among artistic shapes, and the invasion of art by caricature seems to have had at that time the same indirect effect that the encroachments of the cinema were to have later. On occasion caricature abandoned the comic element in favour of an exaggeration which was not far from the world of dreams, and numerous details of the prints of that time remind us of Ensor. Attached as it might try to be to the real, its scope of operations did not entirely break free from that of the Carnival or from the masks of Italian comedy. But to Goya caricature was much more than a setting free of an Italianizing aesthetic (even as regards its dream element), much more than an influence, it was his raw material, just as the newspaper was to be to Balzac, who would bring his genius to light by shedding his transfiguring rays on the items in the news. This raw material, however, could not become art except by becoming a style, and the styles which were respected at the time were opposed to the distortion which Italy conceded alone, and belatedly, to the fantastic. The drawings in which Leonardo has attempted what we now call caricature show only too clearly how remote the spirit of the great Italian style was from it; they seem not so much to be making faces ugly, comic, or typical as to be beautifying and ennobling mis-shapen profiles. They are but exercises in which Leonardo systematically exaggerates sometimes a nose, sometimes a chin, without altering the other features. Often it is only necessary to cover up the distorted feature (here, the chin) to regain the nobility of the profile. When he draws a striking head it is not to express a vice or a blemish but to bring out the power of a condottiere. Rome and Alexandria had attempted something similar in

'*We are Twelve.*' Contemporary caricature

their minor arts but the result had been less noble and just as limited. Certainly classical art, at least in its minor aspects, had divined the harmony in which the apparently discordant features of deformity are united, had realized that the hunch-back, too, has his mask. But the discovery meant little to it, for it did not judge its grotesques and every viable caricature is the expression of a judgement; great political caricature is the work of the opponents of the mighty one whom it portrays.

The caricature which was multiplying then was only a method of drawing and a method is never enough to create a style (otherwise the illustrators of weekly papers would be masters); to sketch coiffures three feet tall because you consider that some are too high is only amusing on occasion, and the caricature of the fashions of the Directory does not go beyond a satire on social vanity. That of manners could go further (with Daumier, the friend of Michelet, it has a content which is political and more or less Christian) but it did not do so of its own accord. In imaginative painting character is inseparable from an ethical message. India did not know this either in its Brahman or its Moslem art; Bosch and Bruegel, as soon as ever they recognize it are moralists; in Gothic painting, especially German, the person characterized is the evil-doer. Every caricature of manners must be based on virtue. Hence a connexion can exist between it and the Devil; whether he appears or not, he

The English in Paris. Contemporary caricature

The Author Hissed. Contemporary caricature

The Wings of the Opera House. Detail from a contemporary caricature

is represented in it by his creatures. But if he adopts a style in it, it is the style of the God who pursues him. The satire of Hogarth's painting, because it is based on a protestant sentimentalism, finds its expression in a sentimental style, as does also the rage of Sade. Goya, who had at one time turned out grotesques similar to those of Leonardo, either went beyond this moral style, ignored it, or actively destroyed it because his indictment rose up from depths very much less clear than those of the 'virtue' he was defending.

It is by no means the individual he discovered in caricature that he opposed to classic abstraction, indeed to the 'grotesques' (which still attracted him). In his etchings he was so little concerned with the distinctive character which is created by the stressing of the peculiarities of a face – the peculiarities which when idealized make it most unlike the same face – that for a century biographers have discussed whether this or that maja is or is not the Duchess of Alba; and yet we know her face from the portraits which he painted of her. And when (occasionally) they agree, they base their conclusions not on the resemblance but on some lines in the painter's notebooks. In the creative work of this famous portrait painter how little the face matters! Women here are interchangeable. In the twenty-four plates of the *Caprichos* there is only one face, Goya's own. In these etchings the principal characters, which are not yet mummers and are never persons, are figures of the theatre.

The theatre, from drama to pantomime, was then the great purveyor of dreams, and almost the only one. Hence its power over every representation of the imaginary, a power comparable with that of the cinema over present-day romance. Goya had not forgotten the Italian theatre, fantastic after its fashion. But for Venice the essence of its society lay in its festivals and their decoration, and in spite of Tiepolo it was a far cry from the *Social Game* to the fancy-dress balls which were awaiting the hour when Bonaparte would shatter their last bits of glass and their melancholy pantomime. Goya put his witches in the place of magicians as harmless, as twisted, and as transparent as Venetian chandeliers; Rousseau, exalting nature, had substituted a light opera setting for a tragic one. The first *Caprichos*, their masqueraders, their duennas, and their intrigues are neither reality nor entirely dreams, but rather a Spanish Theatre more complex than that of the tapestries, a make-believe theatre that often retains the gleam of candle-light.

Undoubtedly the Court and the city lent themselves to such an effect. The capes and serenades, the hearses with yellow plumes that passed slowly across the ancient heraldic setting, the beggars like baroque saints, all belonged to it. The Queen pilfered the powder destined for the army fighting against Portugal so as not to see the resources of the State squandered, resources which were lawfully ear-marked for plays and operas. The story would have it that the late king tried to violate his wife's corpse in the midst of the burning tapers and the monks at prayer. In the squares could be seen the *auto sacramental* of the Annunciation; St Michael takes off his black cloak before the Virgin, revealing a ruff and mauve-coloured pinions; she

GILLRAY: '*Playing in Parts*'. Detail from an etching. London, British Museum.
(The pianist is the Prince of Wales's mistress.)

offers him chocolate which he refuses because God the Father has promised him a *paella* for breakfast, the Holy Ghost enters and all three celebrate their agreement in a most immodest fandango before the astounded ambassadors.

Feelings were expressed at this time by the demonstrative gesture used in the pantomime, where it took the place of words, and in the theatre, where the actor had to allow for the distance between himself and the audience. We have been freed from it by the cinema. There are few such gestures in the *Caprichos,* and later, none. Goya preferred the puppet to the actor.

There had always been something of the puppet about Spanish dress; when its age-old stiffness was allied with clothes which were light but cut in straight lines and with the coiffure of the period, this became, perhaps, even more obvious. Perhaps there was something of it in the Duchess of Alba too. Or has Goya imposed his style upon her? He painted Isabel de Porcel quite differently.

But these puppets are as yet diffident creatures. As everywhere they have their types, often those of the traditional theatre, Celestine with the frog's head, the lady of fashion with the head of a doll; and the series of comic characters that could still be seen ten years ago as one sat in the cafés of little towns in front of some emblazoned church wall behind which red baroque saints crush their torches on altars where hang old blackened swords of military leaders. The male type runs from that of the foolish seducer to those of the miser, the suspect monk, and the waggish gnome, until it is lost in cocked-hatted shadows, the devil's representatives hovering over pairs of women.

Because emotions at this time were portrayed by that which faces had in common, the movements which expressed them in an extreme form, the 'expressive heads' – Fear, Joy, Sadness – played an important part in the teaching of drawing. But the faces of Goya's terrified women scarcely show fear. To touch the spectator by portraying the emotion felt by the subject is one of the rules of baroque aesthetic; in the *Caprichos* there is little but fantastic shapes for the expression of violent emotions. Scenes of fainting martyrs were then in their glory, but Goya's art no longer expresses either the grief or the passion of living beings but rather their nature. The unmoved faces of his women pursued by monsters, the carnival distortion of his monsters themselves, of his gallants, his flirts, his go-betweens, his monks, his witches, all tend towards masquerade. So much is openly portrayed in the *Genealogy*; it comes to life in the riders with animal heads in '*How they tear her*'; lastly the human body disappears and the symbolic asses in the *Caprichos* call to mind a dinner-party of heads. But the animal is the baroque aspect of the masquerade; it is the monkey, beloved of the century, in a Spanish version. Goya did some engravings of it; after it acquired human characteristics it gradually disappears from his work or takes fantastic forms. The alarming flying dog replaces the laughing ass; on the wall of the House of the Deaf Man there was to be a back view of the satanic he-goat.

41

LEONARDO DA VINCI: *Caricature.*
Windsor Castle, Royal Library

Already the aggravation of life expressed in caricature was giving way to a deeper and more uneasy feeling; often the border-line between the face and that which is taking its place is no longer discernible. The young woman in the second capricho is wearing a velvet mask but what of the old woman who follows her? Is she wearing a mask or are we looking at her features?

The mask was not in Goya's view something which hid the face but that which determined it. All great arts (Babylonian, Precolumbian, Chinese, Roman), when they dealt with the Devil, belonged to the mask in some degree. But had its use spread in the eighteenth century? To be sure, and at Venice

first of all. The domino was worn for amusement, for intrigue, and for protection from the sun. Goya forgot it after a few plates and then, when he wanted to fix the features of the living, rediscovered the true mask which is nothing but the face of the dead.

Did he realize this? Probably not. Experts have taken a long time to discover the underground tunnels that connect the Mardi Gras of today with the world of the departed. But if Goya knew nothing of the offspring of the supernatural he was only too well aware of its parentage. Others have become mediums on recovering from dreadful illnesses, Goya brought back from his an aura of the other world which worried and perplexed him more than it frightened him; but it also called in question the world from which he had stood aloof. His demons were his familiars, as are their tamed monsters to the clowns who make

Alexandrian Grotesque. Paris, Louvre

42

GOYA: *The Nightmare*. Drawing.
Madrid, Prado

them do their tricks; but he knew that they were familiars only to him and that they still had the power of casting a spell over people. His art consists of controlling their appearances and taming madness so as to make a language of it. He is fully aware of the force of that language, he may not know whence it comes but he recognizes the accent of the eternal in it.

Even so his connexion with the demon is still ambiguous. He takes care to say

GOYA: '*No one knows himself.*' Etching. (Capricho 6)

that 'every work of his art is a synthesis'. His drawing is indeed synthetic, and sometimes passionately so. What of his characters? It is true enough of his married people and his traditional Celestines. But are his demons a compound of all the devils he has seen? 'Painting makes its choice from the universal', he answers well enough. Nevertheless, the invention of a comic type requires one method, that of a monster drawn from the collective unconscious quite another.

GOYA: Detail from Capricho 2: '*They say Yes, etc.*' Etching

The demon, even more than masks, attracts monsters. Goya discovered them afresh. They had held an enormous position in art and it had needed Greece to free the world from them. They had accompanied rather than expressed Eastern religion and had died with it. Christianity had known devils, but they are not representations; they are satires. It is surprising that in Christian art Satan is universally laughable; monster for monster, a spider with a human face in a hole, or an octopus spreading its tentacles would have far surpassed in horror the figures we know. But would the Church have permitted them? Would she not have concluded that such sights imply an unbearable contact with the powers of darkness? She would hardly agree to a figure of the demon which did not imply the cleansing of him who had conceived it; and she would tolerate no collusion unless it was conscious.

45

GOYA: *Detail from 'Genealogy'.*
Etching. (Capricho 57)

GOYA: Detail from the drawing for Capricho 40:
'Of what illness will he die?'

For ages Spain had felt herself to be an abettor of the higher diabolism. Philip II
had peopled the vistas of the catacombs that guarded his solitude with the creations
of Bosch. And who but Bosch and Bruegel had forestalled Goya in summoning
such convincing monsters from unplumbed depths? And Bruegel did not surpass
the vividness of the Temptations until, in the *Dulle Griet* he met the Scourge, the
maddened slut let loose in a fiery, seething mass of misery. But like him and like
Bosch, Goya seemed not to hear anything now but the murmuring of his secret
language. What he did understand was that his enemy was the Creation. Following
the Flemish diabolists he fought against it with a satirical fantasy. He knew now –
and he was the first to know it for three hundred years – that his world would never
replace the real one except by a new system of relationships between things and
beings. Bosch painted men-houses, demon-fish, roundel-hats and gave life to their
strange world by thrusting it into time, by giving crutches to his devils (wounded in
what battles?), and by plunging it in space; the damned, made of shellfish and egg-
shells, fall for ever into the depths of a background that Bosch was picturing at about
the same time as Leonardo was working; they fall in a hellish evening as clear as the
twilight of our infancy, in a hellish night in which, behind the sad face of Mankind,

46

GOYA: *Goblins*. Etching. (Capricho 49)

there turn windmills with sails of fire, a night more charged with poetry than the burning of Rome.

Goya, for his part, represents a simpleton being shaved by women who skin him, adds to carnival the mummery of the Inquisition; tired of putting masks on his characters he turns the face into a mask, or into an animal, or replaces it with an animal's head; gives asses human gestures; combines man and beast for his *Sorcerers Out Walking*; invents the Chinchilla, a man with padlocks for ears; dis-

47

PIETER BRUEGEL: '*Dulle Griet*' (*Mad Meg*). Detail. Antwerp, Musée Royal

covers the spectral voice of draped figures clothing themselves in the void; enlarges
the hands of the *Goblins*. Life is given to all this by its irony and by the appearance
in an unusual setting of familiar sentiments which snatch these scenes out of the
moment and extend them in a life of their own; sorcerers and demons must cut
their nails; ghosts watch for the coming of day so that they can flee in time. But
Goya disposed also of an obscure people that the Flemish had not known – a
people which was not, strictly speaking, imagined but rather intercepted. Did he

48

Bosch: *Hell*. Detail from the *Garden of Earthly Delights*. Madrid, Prado

PIETER BRUEGEL: 'Dulle Griet' (Mad Meg). Detail. Antwerp, Musée Royal

himself distinguish between the monsters that he owed to the combinations taken from a revived tradition, the *Sorcerers Out Walking* for example, and those brought to him from the depths of ages by sleep and especially by dreaming. The enormous hand of the *Goblins*, and the clothes without a face are well known to psycho-analysts; the plucked man-chicken is one of the strange beasts that they are still discussing and one which the unconscious seems to bring up from its deepest depths. Saturn has always been the god of witchery.

Caricaturists in all humility want to reduce the world to one single meaning, to reveal what it hides by isolating it from what is hidden; Goya wanted to extend it, to add that which would prolong it into the regions of mystery. He does not illuminate it like a moralist, a pamphleteer, or a satirist; the light which he lets down, instead of illuminating the puppets, stretches their immense shadows out over infinity. In his time Bosch and Bruegel were counted among the caricaturists (as Baudelaire was to count them later); the distortion which was decisively breaking away from reality had already learnt how to get back to the supernatural.

Stylized as the art of this period may have been, and in spite of Fragonard and David, illusion – the 'objective vision', it may be, of the imaginary – played a pre-eminent part in it. The modesty of caricature freed it from this. Being a two-dimensional art, like those of the ante-classical era, it did not attempt to compete with the real while it resembled it. It still, however, remained obedient to it. But if we look at the first *Caprichos* after seeing an album of contemporary caricatures we are gripped by the presence of a new dimension which is by no means that of depth.

Of course there is a *kind* of depth in the *Caprichos*, but it is not that of 'reality', or that of the Italians (Goya's distance is not an horizon). It is a depth of lighting – which caricature did not possess, consisting as it did of lines or low relief, sometimes coloured in flat tints. Nor does Goya's lighting tend to build up space. Like that of Rembrandt, and of the cinema, it tends to connect that which it marks off from the shadow

GOYA: *Sorcerers Out Walking: 'See how solemn they are.'* Etching. (Capricho 63)

and to give it a meaning that goes beyond it, and, to be precise, transcends it. The darkness is not merely black, it is also darkness.

*

Again, the work to which this lighting gives all its effect destroyed that which for several centuries had allowed the artist to make the severest object decorative and even the very symbol of harmony; I mean the arabesque. Since the close of the Gothic era it had existed everywhere. Baroque art had many times broken the continuous line favoured by the men of the Renaissance but its own most broken line remained obedient to the hidden curves of a world which longed to be voluptuous or ornate. We speak, rightly, of the strength and freedom of Goya's world. But lines and strokes were becoming more and more free; his freedom, as early as the tapestries, was only getting back to that of Fragonard. For all that, the freest strokes of Fragonard were still guided by the calligraphy which he made his painting obey. Let us only contrast the mouths of his women with those of Goya's. He expresses the values of his time, Goya destroys them. Goya alone introduced the abandonment of the highest form of the arabesque, the sinuosity instinctively bestowed on the

Detail from a contemporary caricature

female nude. To the artists of the time that had been the decisive victory over the Middle Ages. The fluting of draperies among which this was achieved, far from being a 'perception', corresponded to the negroes with scimitars in Byzantine painting; it was a means of bringing the profane into contact with the sacred. However mechanical the medieval line had become it had always endeavoured to express the separation of man from the divine. The arabesque expressed their coming together. That is why Spanish baroque – the baroque of a country where man had not been 'reconciled' with God and Hell always existed – retained in sculpture so many Gothic planes; and why, when it was defeated by the Italian style, it

Nadie nos ha visto.

GOYA: '*No one has seen us.*' Etching. (Capricho 79)

tried to release itself with the help of hair, swords, and blood. Goya re-introduced into painting the sword and blood, and that 'realism' that begins with the beggar and ends with the ghost. And he fell in with the only Western genius who had antici-pated him in raising a universe of the imagination in opposition to the shape which the Italian Renaissance had imposed on the dreams of mankind – Rembrandt.

The line that Goya was trying to grasp by means of nightmares, the line that would free from the theatre the human form, the setting of a picture, and the world, is almost Rembrandt's. Rembrandt had in effect invented a new method of picture-making. Apart from some of Titian's works which most probably he never saw, Rembrandt had been the first to abandon outline. It is said that he put light in its place; rather, he put a field of expressive signs in the place of illusion. He seems to have worked 'from inside'. Far from seeking the delineation of *characters*, like Michelangelo or Tintoretto, he had fled from it in his own way. It is true that his etchings have a light of destiny crossing them, but often we are thinking about his etchings when we are talking about the sepia drawings; they are as different from them as they are from his pictures. He etched with a point but drew with a brush. Even so, he did not always free himself from the arabesque. It seems to have gone

REMBRANDT: *The Three Crosses*. First state of the etching

from the last state, bitten and re-bitten, of the *Three Crosses*; but it had been evident in the foreground figures of the earlier states, and, in etchings of as rich a style as *Jesus shown to the People*, had unexpectedly embellished some character with a plumed head-dress. Rembrandt often broke it and put a jagged line in place of its continuous curve, but still he supported its appeal to a dressed-up world. How far does Goya thrust aside, in military uniforms, everything that would have allowed him to find again the baroque of helmets and galleys! Even under the barred rays of a tempest the simplification of a tree in Rembrandt results in curves; in Goya, it ends in their removal and in the presence of a rock. There is in some of Rembrandt's later work, the *Mocking of Christ* for instance, a line that is crushed, stretched, and to all appearances diffident – this diffident line was going to change the whole world's method of drawing! – which Goya does not seem to have known; a line which Picasso would revive in some of the *Tumblers*, and which owes nothing to

REMBRANDT: *The Three Crosses*. Last state of the etching

arabesque; however, Rembrandt's etching technique had produced such a print as the *Prodigal Son*. Goya took up the process where Rembrandt had left it. He also worked for preference with a brush; he also was looking for a particular revelation; he also was less intent on face than on movement, less on movement than on the setting, less on the setting than on a complicated dramatic message whose unity produces the unity of the print or the picture and creates for him a work of art. With him would die the solemn mass in which the Biblical light transfigures the people of its master; Goya had no light, only illumination.

The reason is that the world of Rembrandt and his disciples was as ordered and as hierarchically organized as that of the great Venetians though its order is less of this world than is that of his contemporaries Velazquez and Poussin; all his eddies of shadow converge towards a single brilliant spot – God. His language was the language of the prophets of the Tradition, it swept away the vainglorious edifices of man so that the supreme order might appear in its majesty; the shining face that calms the sea, and sheds at last on all living things, as on all the pitiful creations of the artist, light and pity. Goya also was a prophet, *but he did not know precisely of what.*

In his cartoons volumes had been expressed at first by melting lines which detached them from the hazy distances of tapestry. The backgrounds of his pictures had also been conventional, except that of the *Meadow of San Isidro*. Those of his

58

etchings consist of indistinct trees or of scattered fragments, barely suggested, of ghost-towns, and for interiors, of which Rembrandt had been fond, there is at most a window somewhere.

But even so they are not abstract like the backgrounds of caricatures; they provide the Apocalyptic light which unites his couples, his grotesques, his spectres, and his torments. Engraving struggles violently against reality, not only because it disdains colour (no artist of genius liked colour-engraving until modern times) and so involves more uncompromisingly than painting does the rivalry that exists between the artist and the world, but still more because its materials, like that of mosaic, have a character of their own to which the subject represented is foreign. Etching, in-so-far as it is an art, is almost as different from drawing as it is from painting. The wood-engraver and the engraver on metal see what they are engraving, the etcher hardly ever does. The material to which he attaches such importance only appears with the proofs; he engraves a negative and instead of *composing* a picture must imagine it. Of course, etching is not an uncanny art; but no technique agrees better with the uncanny than it does. It is the replacing of the background peculiar

REMBRANDT: *The Prophet Elisha and the Shunamite*. Drawing. Bayonne, Musée Bonnat

59

GOYA: '*And still they don't go away.*' Preparatory drawing. Madrid, Prado

GOYA: '*And still they don't go away.*' Etching. (Capricho 59)

GOYA: '*When day comes, we must be off.*' Etching. (Capricho 71)

to tapestry by that peculiar to engraving which permits Goya's figures to find their emphasis. His tapestry background had upheld a tradition; the aquatint background that he discovered, like the density of the high-lights in the *Meadow*, shut out the illusionist colour-blendings which animated his characters. He inserts his sketches in a coherently modelled universe and forces their lines into a style; this material which expresses reality without imitating it calls for a method of drawing which expresses reality without imitating it, a method which itself takes its value from its material, from its thick or scratched line, from the break in its arabesque, from everything which makes it an *engraved line*. The resin dust brings him a world at once imaginary and remote – the other world. His patches of dark colour often seem to represent darkness but their function is more like that of the golden backgrounds of the Middle Ages; they take the scene out of reality and, as with the Byzantine scene, place it at once in a universe that does not belong to man. This black is devil's gold; it marks out the fantastic as strictly as the golden background had marked out the sacred. It is very rare in the preparatory designs, even when they are in ink, but nearly always it interposes itself to give the engraving its disturbing emphasis and to remove the scene into the supernatural.

Goya did not intend to achieve this supernatural element by means of a flat background in harmony with a hieratic style, but by broken lines similar to those of Europe. Byzantium was far away and Romanticism very close. His genius consists in understanding that a method of drawing that disdained illusion and was indifferent to Italian conventionalism, when allied to an illumination which rejected that vision and that conventionalism, had nothing to do with the imitation of illumined characters or with an exact representation of colours or values, but everything to do with the search for means (of which the chief was aquatint) as little concerned with illusion as sepia. It is no accident that so many masters of the supernatural, great colourists as they are, end by abandoning colour, nor that almost all are engravers.

The black background of aquatint demanded a ruggedness of composition that painting had never known. Goya would in the end replace the decorative style, the light of the *Meadow*, with the almost haggard manner of the *Madhouse*, and find in it, failing a Revelation, the entreaty of Islam, the *cante jondo* with which the mountains of Aragon still resound, the breathless and ponderous accent which the East acquires in Spain. After the flirts, puppets, marionettes, masks, animals, and friendly demons, the ghosts look up at the vast tombstone that is going to bury them. This plate was the first summons of the powerful voice from beneath the earth. If only the demons, their little arms upraised, would flee in the dawn! It is not daylight that is coming, it is the end of satire, the accent of incurable night.

GOYA: *The Manikin.* Madrid, Prado

'YDIOMA UNIVERSAL'

THERE was an element of discretion in the word *Caprichos*, as in the preface that he prefixed to it and in the gift to the king of the copper plates of the album. But not in the assertion by Goya that he was a satirist. He believed it, but was he a satirist of politicians, men about town, coquetry, doctors, preachers, and aristocratic pride? Rather it was of everything which he considered imposture. Undoubtedly the scope of the great humorists always seems rather limited, including even that of Molière. But Molière's genius was neither a religious nor a metaphysical one and he only wanted to do away with the comic side of man in society; his myth was the real man. Undoubtedly, his etchings finished with, Goya had the idea that they were aimed at man, even real man; not man in society but Mankind itself – beginning with woman.

Of the satires to which he laid claim that on woman is the most suspect. For twenty years he had treated her as a decorative personality. Then she becomes a mask. In his etchings he portrays her (when she is young) in the exercise or preparation of deceit; when she is old she becomes the giver of evil advice, the procuress, the witch. If men and women cease to meet for preposterous display, abduction and rape take its place. More than towards rape which, in the later *Disasters*, belongs especially to brutality, he inclines towards a complicated group of phantasms (which Laclos and Sade also knew) where each sex takes violent possession of the other. It extends from the timid *Pelele* of the tapestries to the maddened subjects of the *Disparates* by way of the man skinned by the female barbers, of men-chickens whom women pluck and spit or chase with brooms, and women-chickens plucked in their turn and eaten. But the latter, who follow the others like a caricature of punishment, are eaten by men-animals of a rather abstract kind while the young women with the skewer are the most human figures in the whole collection in that they are the only ones where the face expresses a complex emotion – to be precise, sadistic pleasure. Woman was now for Goya the heiress of Genesis, the potential witch, the creature possessed by the unknown world.

Anyone who wishes to understand the art of this period would be well advised to study the eroticization of the nude. Goya employed it rarely, went beyond it, and invented animalization; the world of demons has always known the beast.

Western civilization saw so clearly that the *raison d'être* of art lay in a pleasure that began with participation and ended in delight that it did not realize that it had held that belief for less than two centuries. Yet the process that transformed a nude by Poussin into one by Fragonard was by no means clear. People saw in either case nudes which they delighted to imagine as creatures of flesh and blood; but the

65

devil neglected the standing nudes of Poussin, not Boucher's women prone on their stomachs. The *Nude Maja* is for Goya inseparable from the *Draped Maja;* she is an undressed woman who, without in any way looking at the spectator, is aware of him. She calls attention to the least physiological aspect of sex, her personality. (I have written elsewhere that for analysing the erotic relationship between Madame de Rênal and Julien Sorel, Stendhal would have had at his disposal a more subtle equipment than he needed for the artlessly military pages of his journal...) Painters have noticed that in the *Nude Maja* the nude seems ill-adapted to the head. Ten years earlier dilettanti were substituting the engraved face of Marie-Antoinette for those on erotic prints... Painting had known several nudes of personalities, as opposed to sublimated females, but here for the first time it recognized something quite different from Boucher's innocently licentious display, the stripping of a slave-queen whose hostile look remains. Underlying a Poussin nude, there is contemplation; underlying a Rembrandt, the everlasting; an eighteenth-century French nude suggests only complicity in rape.

The *Nude Maja* is a nude without precedent. It is absurd to see in it a repetition of the *Toilet of Venus* by Velazquez. Certainly the latter is the first goddess become woman and therefore of an outstanding historical importance. Goya was not the

Velazquez: *Venus*. London, National Gallery

first to paint a nude with personality, he was the first to paint a nude who should be erotic without being voluptuous.

The *Draped Maja* is a recumbent portrait, one among other admirable recumbent portraits; the *Nude* is certainly not one among others. No more the heir to the Venuses of Titian than to the innocent Velazquez, it is more alluring than they are but with a different kind of allurement. The Venetian nudes disown their robes, the *Nude Maja* has thrown hers off. In her, sexuality is no longer the lyrical call to possession of the world through living beings; participation in her loneliness is what this little Byzantine nocturne has to offer. To see how well the arabesque suits sensual delight it is enough to compare Velazquez' nude with Goya's; in the latter the line, like the line in his future drawings, suddenly becomes glowing and, as it were, hammered out.

Goya's nudes are few. His erotic fancy was happier with women in chains, or bound by some devil. The seductive sketch in the Prado, so modern and so troubled, has still some subtle hint of the Gothic about it, but of a Gothic that does not know the Mother. (Goya writes with surprise, beneath a sketch of a woman carrying a child: 'This one has the look of a good woman . . .'). His art, which had only to pass from portrait to invention to become cruel, was erotically austere. He was attached to what he suggested, not to what he depicted.

The series of *Mirrors* (which look like sketches for the *Caprichos* and which were never engraved) springs from an almost commonplace idea; people look at themselves in a glass which reflects their caricature. One man sees a monkey, another a cat, but a third sees his collar changed into a garrotte. A young woman sees the scythe of time with a snake entwined round the haft. An obvious symbol, but at her side an astonished man beholds a frog which is no longer entirely a symbol and does not resemble him. Goya returned to the frog later, and the man. The frog remained and the man disappeared. His shadowy outline can be seen only partly blotted out from right to left, then there is a new version on which the belt can be seen, and lastly another version. On the last figure, which is going towards the frog, there has been added in ink (the drawing was done with a brush) the chastity belt, as studied as the contrivances of Leonardo. Later still Goya took up the subject again. Now the belt passes to the frog, that is, to the woman. (The obstacle will be the same . . . and the frog was initially the reflection of the man.) The two figures are now brought so close together that they caress one another and the man has become a monster. Goya has passed from facetiousness to the ante-chamber of mystery.

Molière is far away . . . How slight are his characters' absurdities when confronted by Spain, the heir to the visions of Don Quixote!

It would be unwise to attempt a close analysis of the means by which this delving beneath the surface was effected but we can at least observe it in process. Sometimes it plays on elementary symbols. The *Old Women* look at themselves in a mirror but they are themselves what the *Young Women (Majas Out Walking)*, who are not looking, should see, and Time that sweeps them up has taken the place of the scythe in the earlier drawing. Sometimes more complex methods were employed than the symbol, after the double faces of the *Dream of Fickleness*. In the sexual sphere satire had hitherto often dealt with lewdness, that is to say, excess; Goya aims at sex itself; 'On the absurdity of being human'.

Our age has made it its business to interpret this jeer; it is the jeering of the condemned. There is wit in the courtyards which lead to execution; an ironical attitude similar to Goya's. Although his work was meant for no one but himself a haunting feeling unites his (apparently) most widely differing sketches in a unity of the prison-house – the *feeling of subjection*. Hence the monkey discerned in the mirror, and the cat, and the frog; hence the scythe of Time, but hence also his wings in the drawing where his face has disappeared and where he is binding the hands of the young woman he is going to violate. In the *Caprichos* (I take them one by one) it is implicit

GOYA: *Nude Maja*. Madrid, Prado

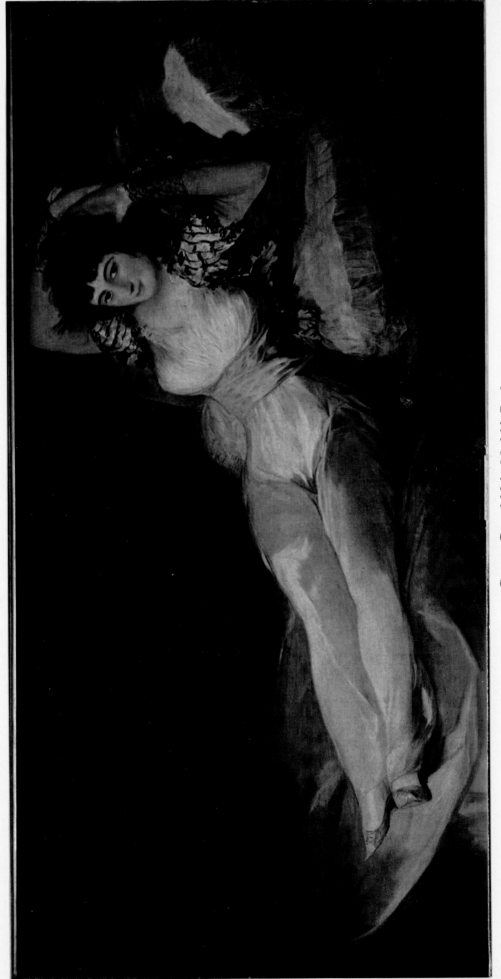

GOYA: *Draped Maja.* Madrid, Prado

GOYA: *The Frog*, first version. Drawing. Madrid, Prado

in the woman who has been carried off, the fainting woman in the *Tantalus*, the lover of the murdered man, the woman desired by the freaks, the woman devoured, the female prisoner, the plucked men, those condemned by the Inquisition, the beaten child, the foetuses carried off by the Weird Sisters, the men with padlocks for ears, the panic-stricken people, the idiots who worship parrots, and in the couple who, fettered by love, are being trampled on by the demon owl.

Engraving, in an age when it was regarded as a minor art, gave to the supernatural world called up by this disturbing message an accent of the fantastic and irresponsible. The masked art by which, in the name of the temporary, Goya tried to reach the everlasting, permitted him to slip through the narrow door in the 'street of Disillusion, with its storeroom of perfumes and liquors, price 320 reals', his first mission to the shades.

73

GOYA: *The Frog*, second version. Drawing. Madrid, Prado

The mask was not merely dictated by prudence. Goya was no outcast painter, no hunted Baudelaire. He painted the king in bed, slept (at fifty years of age) with a pretty duchess, wrestled with farriers. If he painted cats well, he engraved them as though he was not Goya. No one was more blind to the world of cloud, sea, and the moon . . . His haunted destiny was an imperious one, and the Court which was filled with his name glitters for us lit by the rays of his black sun. But he was uncertain how far he was entitled to his phantoms, and still more uncertain how far his phantoms were entitled to enter the domain of art. He waited twenty years before giving them, in paint, their tyrannous accent. Of course, he meant to impose his universe, but he wanted to justify it also; after all, madmen and the Carnival existed. In painting, the fantastic was in a minor category; had it become frightful or horrible

GOYA: *The Frog*, third version. Drawing. Madrid, Prado

GOYA: *Sketch of a Nude*. Madrid, Prado

76

GOYA: Drawing without title. Madrid, Prado

it would have been put in a forbidden one. Goya could not raise this prohibition except by using his art in the attempt to destroy, not the art of reality, but the art of what was then called the ideal.

*

He knew that the time was coming when his universe and the dying lustre of Italy would clash. It cannot be doubted that Spanish artists were impatient of the influence exercised by Italian art. They had come to terms with the baroque ecstasies where sensuality and spirituality met; but in Italy they met in sensuality whereas Spain had always wanted to unite them in God. Imagine St. Teresa before her statue by Bernini . . . It was a strange match; on the one side Italy, which had made the nude the very symbol of art, on the other Spain, where it was punished by a year's imprisonment, banishment, and confiscation of property and where the only nude to come down to us was painted – by the greatest painter of his time, Velazquez – almost in secret, and thanks to royal favour. If Italy had been aiming for centuries to bring man into harmony with himself, the aim of Spain had been to put him at variance. To the 'Christ, man made perfect' of Nicholas of Cusa all the deep voices in Spain replied that man's only worth lay in what he owed to Christ. Goya certainly did not take up the search for these pointers towards divinity, but for him, as for the Middle Ages, man had little value except to the extent that he expressed that which surpasses him. In spirit Spain had remained Gothic; many of her popular artists sought to stamp each person with the mark that joined him to God, and to make their community of characters the heir to what the Christian community of the statues had been.

From its highest talent to its meanest representative, the art of the Court, often foreign, had freed itself from this craving; but to Goya's mind the soul of Spain was no longer to be found at Court. Little did it matter that Venice, which was also dying, had bequeathed to him its domino. In the twilight where the shade of Harlequin was fading, the blood-red Saturn was beginning to rise, just as the tireless denunciations of Sade were sweeping away the bands of elegant romancers. If for him, as for the most enduring genius of his country, man's sole purpose was to bear witness to that which surpassed him, that which surpassed him was no longer God. And Saturn must give an answer, not to the Venetians, but to the spirit of the Sistine – on pain, for Goya, of being merely another Magnasco.

But this could not be done without a feeling of uneasiness, for he believed himself to be a rationalist. 'The Sleep of Reason brings forth monsters.' That is why, no doubt, he later covered his walls with them. His notes to the *Caprichos* assert that the scenes depicted are the result of superstition and poor education. It is wrong to believe in ghosts. Why, then, paint them so convincingly? We are reminded of

GOYA: *The Duchess of Alba*. Private Collection

79

Laclos proclaiming about the same time the moral nature of the *Liaisons Dangereuses*. At the end of the *Disasters* an odd-looking puppet, puppet and Reason at one and the same time, just as the Duchess of Alba of the *Caprichos* is both puppet and Duchess, brings forward, in all the pomp of Jesuit trappings, a symbol of appeasement. After which Goya engraved *An old man straying among phantoms* . . . He was seeking the style that suited his genius and not one to suit his moral teaching. He was a rationalist in the same way that Cervantes was a writer of adventure stories and Dostoievsky a novelist on social themes. The rationalism of his notes to the *Caprichos* is moralizing, but almost all the prophets of the irremediable – to whatever degree they are such – set themselves up as moralists: Pascal, Baudelaire, Dostoievsky, Tolstoy, Nietzsche . . .

Again, nothing is superior to morality for conferring the right to introduce cruelty. Look at Hogarth. Sade himself claimed to be a moralist, and a rationalist. He used his appeals to reason, as Goya used some brief sentences and several figures of Justice, to justify his constant listening to the voices of blood and darkness, which are not concerned with justification, and what he conjures up retains the tone adopted by other moralists for bleating. A novelist, he has access through the medium of his narrative to the ambiguity of fictitious conversation, for which painting has no equivalent; but his season in Hell, which lasted nearly all his life, recounted in a tone sometimes descending to the maudlin makes us long, alas, to rewrite it. Imagine *Juliette* written in the clear tones of Laclos, or Diderot; or in the breathless accents that Michelet was to bring so often from the provinces of Goya.

Goya did not intend to come back from Hell and speak with the voice of others. But what he had to overcome – something Sade accepted – was at once a style and the shape of a civilization. And if Fragonard counted for less than Rousseau, Raphael counted for more than Racine. Neither Guardi, Hogarth, Boucher, nor Chardin copied Raphael but none of them considered himself the equal of the great Italians. The painting of this period wrote *Candide* while reverencing *Zaïre*. Its brilliance was too closely allied to taste not to be threatened by the saturation of sensibility that fashion inexorably brings. But as soon as art became ambitious again, its ambition centred on values it had never questioned. It passed from light verse to Chénier's 'burning night', from Greuze's pretty faces to his Roman profiles, from the early Fragonard to his cameo-like faces. Winckelmann owed his sudden popularity to something besides his talent. Boucher had been one of the teachers of the only contemporary painter that Goya called great – David.

To what extent the entire period believed that every accomplishment should take an 'antique' form is amply demonstrated by the vocabulary of the French Revolution. These children of Rousseau wanted to speak like those of Plutarch. The platform was more suited to that than was painting – but painting suited it fairly well. The return of the supernatural, which was then almost as insistent as the exaltation of feeling, seemed to bring into an ornate world an intrusion of phantoms which soon copied its style. Classical tragedy had certainly known how to dress the Furies. The ghosts of the age would soon be leaving their loneliness behind; the years stretching from the guillotine in the Place de la Révolution to the snows of the field of Eylau would see to that . . . But their call was stifled, and its constant repetition all in vain so long as it produced only the setting of a castle haunted by classical spectres. It appeared self-evident that the Italian style of composition expressed the supreme excellence of line. It has been said that Goya was freed from it by his romantic material, his monsters, and his witches. But his contemporary Fuseli, whose material is often so close to his own (*The Nightmare*, the *Three Witches*, etc.) shows us that witches can be painted Louis XVI or Empire; and the taste of the period would gladly have imposed the 'antique' style on the most confused obsessions, just as it was beginning to impose it on sensuality. Fuseli wanted to refine his witches in a rational manner. An odd idea; but what did Goya want? To make reproductions of mad old women? He did not mean to endow his fantastic world with a lower *quality* than Fuseli intended to give to his; but in order to make his witch into a work of art he was not satisfied to make her into a Pythian priestess.

FUSELI: *The Nightmare*. Brush drawing. London, British Museum

What had engraving brought him? The end of illusion and seduction; the discovery that man could be taken out of himself by other means than beauty and that the effect of the supernatural lies not in its representation but in its style; and the certainty that the supernatural first, and then the human, are less expressible by specific means in the assumed service of representation than by a representation in the service of a style and of the means employed by that style.

Some of his work reveals how he groped his way forward; the fantastic figures of the *Alameda*, for instance, and especially of the *Brocken*, an elaborate Capricho. His cartoons all belong to the art of illusion; each of them, could it become real, would turn out to be a spectacle. He had tried first of all to apply this scrupulous kind of art to the fantastic, to represent the aerial dance of *real* witches above a figure from a fresco similar to the characters in *Winter* or the *Well*. But when he painted the *Madhouse* he discovered convincingly that the way to express the unusual, the frightening, that is, the inhuman, was not to attempt the careful representation of a spectacle, real or imaginary, but to use a treatment capable of representing it without yielding to its component parts.

GOYA: *The Brocken.*
Madrid, Duke of Osuña collection

It was the discovery of the very meaning of style; and, at the same time, of the peculiar strength of painting, of the power of a broken line or the bringing together of a red and a black over and above the demands of the objects represented. Vision has been mentioned; but the vision of the *Madhouse* is not more accurate or more acute than that of the *Brocken*. It is not the vision that has become peremptory but the execution. The shadow under the arm of the walking figure is not a shadow but an accent. Egyptian art had discovered the style to express the everlasting but it had not discovered vision; in the same way, at the opposite extreme of the methods used by man, Goya transferred from engraving to painting the style proper to anguish.

Try to imagine the spectacle

painted in the *Brocken*; it will not be very different from the picture. Try to imagine the *Madhouse*. You can recall without difficulty the walking figure, the individual with the feathers, and the singer; but their emphasis is quite different from that in the picture; they are separated from the other figures; that in the right background has disappeared, on the left a crowd, horrible in a commonplace way, has taken the place of the haunted swarming mass. Even when imagined with exactness the madman with the crown loses that which compels our admiration.

Let us go further and suppose that a film director had to shoot this scene. Even before placing his characters he will realize that he cannot attempt to approach Goya's genius except by the use of lighting – not to give the figures he is going to photograph as much reality as possible but to veil them in the semi-darkness of tragedy. And the broken stroke which gives its quality to each figure in the picture is the means by which Goya brings them all into harmony with his striking world of *imaginary* light and shade, with a plastic world that has become the expression of madness and not its representation.

Emphatically he was not the inventor of style; he invented his own. Every artist of genius discovers his method of expressing the world at the same time as his style, and not at the same time as his 'vision' – a dubious discovery when the expression seems peculiarly obedient to observation, which is always subordinate to it. El Greco discovered his style when he rejected the evidence of the spectator's senses. Goya spoke of truth because he was opposed to Italian fiction which had been falsified by popularization, as every style is; but he only became Goya when he opposed to the fiction, not reality, but another overpowering fiction; when he opposed to a dressed-up world a world in rags, to a world whose ordering matched its flowers a world ordered according to its roots. He retained from the earlier form of his art its popular models and the scene, the imagined spectacle, though henceforward it was half-way between *reportage* and nightmare. His subjects could have belonged (some do belong) to Magnasco – except the very one of madness. The carnival, even the Inquisition, are spectacles. Madness cannot be one except in-so-far as it is limited to a carnival, as it would have been by Magnasco. In the *Interrogation* the latter depicts a prisoner whose eyes are being burnt out; but he depicts him with such gusto that the torture becomes a kind of ballet. The Italian style comes between the spectator and the torment depicted; Goya, like the Gothic painters, at the same time as he preserves the difference between a work of art and a spectacle of horror, becomes involved in it and involves the spectator in it. The Italian drama stopped at anything which would have overthrown its decorative quality; Goya abolished decoration. Against the sinister, naked walls the madman is no longer a masquerader, he is an accuser.

Ever since the sixteenth century the idea of man formulated in Italy had been questioned only by people on the fringe of society; this is true even of a Teresa of

GOYA: *Plague Hospital*. Madrid, Private Collection

GOYA: *Madhouse.* Madrid, Academy of San Fernando

GOYA: *The Madhouse*. Detail. Madrid, Academy of San Fernando

Avila. And European civilization had not put forward any other against it; the conception of quality in representation, and then even in painting, had been based on a single fundamental idea, that of the Reconciliation between man and God. Ribera's imitation of Caravaggio merely overlaid Spain, by way of Naples, with a harsher form of Italianism. Velazquez had pursued by himself one of the highest enterprises that painting had known, but he had not been opposed to the spirit of the Italian style. The Golden Age, like the age of Louis XIV, accepted the world; and Venice as well. Goya rejected it, and meant to give to his rejection the strength and brilliance that the West had achieved by its acceptance. The Protestant countries had forgotten the old Augustinian accent in order to adapt themselves, more or less successfully, to a rationalist art. Rembrandt alone had opposed to Italianism a domain worthy to be compared with that on which Italian art relied, but Rembrandt had still not inspired an aesthetic. The sole rival to Raphael was Titian.

When we read the words in which Goya proclaims what he owes to Rembrandt we think first of all of the break in the brush stroke. Perhaps he meant more than that. Rembrandt had been the first to set against the 'idealization' of Italian art an art which was equally ambitious. Hals, Velazquez, and Vermeer no doubt thought that they painted better than Raphael but they did not compete with the world of his invention, being – perhaps – indifferent to it. Rembrandt, knowingly or not, and however obsessed he may have been with the specific domain of painting, had attempted in several of his pictures, and several of his etchings, what Aeschylus and Michelangelo had attempted before him. And on occasion he had succeeded, and so transformed his characters that they had been brought into harmony with the light he drew sometimes from Revelation and sometimes from eternity – a light which transcends time like the Biblical moment when the shadow of David's outstretched arms takes the shape of the Cross. It was not to the prophets of Israel that Goya turned, but it was perhaps from Rembrandt that he learnt the supreme accent of an individual universe when that universe contained in itself the oldest feelings known to mankind.

The most widely diffused aesthetic of his times, that of France, seemed self-evident; the painter's function was to represent in a talented manner wonderful or pleasing spectacles. This is what Goya had been doing until he was forty-five. The belief that one admired in painting that which, were it to become real, would have been desirable, certainly appeared to justify both the taste for Raphael and that for Fragonard, but the painters themselves knew that painting was painting and, as simple as Diderot, did not notice the proofs of Rembrandt's genius in their eagerness to follow his characters in the street. Velazquez could not be reduced to what he represented. This Europe, beset as it now was by phantoms, was so convinced that all art which does not seduce must dignify that it hoped, like Fuseli, to tame its phantoms by dignifying them. The Italian discovery, hackneyed as it may have become as a result of praise and imitation, was that art is one of the most powerful forces for adjusting the world, a kingly domain where man escapes from the human state to reach another where he is at one with the gods. The lustre that was Rome's had not come about because its great works adorned man but because they set him free. Goya discovered that if the Italian style can make men into figures of divinity

88

it is art itself which makes the artist a rival of the gods. It is the same whether it embellishes its subject or not, whether it is the art of Velazquez or of Rembrandt; it matters little whether the artist is trying to possess the heavens or the night,

REMBRANDT: *Girl with a broom*. Washington, National Gallery of Art (Mellon Collection)

provided both are deep enough. Goya was not groping towards God, but towards a power older and beyond salvation, the everlasting Saturn.

Another artist of genius, perhaps separated from Christ by the same subterranean voice, had also called upon a people of madmen, sleep-walkers, and witches for the unconquerable accent that before his time had always been a Christian accent – the Shakespeare of Macbeth and Hamlet. The mist that transforms the figures wandering on the heath in Lear is quite different from the murky light in which the out-stretched arms of the pathetic little man of the *Third of May* call upon the Spanish people; but both, when they make their appeal to the powers of darkness, are bent on equalling or surpassing that element of the everlasting which is inherent in classical tragedy and Italian painting. Shakespeare uses characters, Goya figures; but since painting began, what painter but Goya would have been able to realize the depth of the endless corridors around the imagined spot of blood that all the perfumes of Arabia would never wash away?

'In such a night as this, when the sweet wind did gently kiss the trees and they did make no noise . . .' Ah, song of love! In such a night, Macbeth, you heard

'Thou shalt be king', and in such a night the forest marched on Dunsinane. In such a night Saul went to the witch of Endor's cave, Helen saw the first dead of Troy return, and Alexander crucified the philosopher who had taught him wisdom; Rome, Persepolis, Alexandria and Babylon went up in flames, the heiress of Tamerlane cast to the fish in her turquoise pool all the pearls of Samarkand, and the beleaguered companions of Cortez heard the Spanish prisoners shriek when their hearts were torn out to the beating of gongs; in such a night Cervantes learnt that he was a slave.

The vulnerability of all great art of the Italian or Chinese type lies in this, that it takes its stand on a denial of the subterranean element of the divine, an element which one day rises up unconquerable. Whereas Italy had wanted to rescue man from his condition by reducing him to his perfection, just as it made of Christ the perfect man and the dispenser of never-failing forgiveness, Goya wanted to rescue him by finding again the forgotten rumbling of the voices that he heard beneath the generations like the everlasting murmur of the beach beneath the endless beating of the waves. And he knew that he would never express that message by using the

GOYA: Drawing without title. Madrid, Prado

91

Italian style because the Italian style was nothing but the expression of a world where the Devil does not exist.

He transformed the function of painting; no longer was it to be used to beguile the dilettante or to annex an imaginary world by beautifying it. He proclaimed a new right of the painter. Was it the right to madness? Madness fascinated him; he often watched for its approach. Is there not the story that he caught cold in the mountains so as to prove to the Duchess of Alba his skill as a farrier! He knew what syphilis was, and that his intermittent deafness was a silent overture to disaster. Such a madness was not fantasy. What makes the accent of his madmen, his flagellants, and his carnival peremptory is this – it is the age-old religious accent of useless suffering rediscovered, perhaps for the first time, by a man who believed himself to be indifferent to God. But the voice which had begun to people his silence – the silence that would not cease growing deeper – was not merely his own; it was the forgotten voice of Spain.

GOYA: *The Queen of the Circus*. Etching. (Proverbios 20)

DISASTERS

THERE are in the *Disasters* several fantastic or allegorical scenes among the episodes of war and famine. Some would see in these plates the sequel, enriched by twenty years of genius, to those of the *Caprichos* . . . '*They carried her away*' could certainly have appeared in the later plates. But when the scenes of manners disappeared they took with them, beside the element of comedy, the element of caricature that had marked them; the black backgrounds are often replaced by a very coarse-grained aquatint or by close strokes of the pen. There is the precision of the graving tool about the representation of some of the bodies cut in pieces. Lastly a breathless scratching, whose anger far surpasses that of the designs that precede it, has replaced the 'dashed off' accent of the *Caprichos*. The demons have now found their true shape – the horrific. Ever since his illness Goya had been seeking those horrors that the universal anguish of mankind instantly recognizes – humiliation, nightmares, rape, prison. But now his dungeons and tortures were spread over the whole of Spain, and his art had grown worthy to bring together the public confession of a world which shouted what his etchings had whispered.

Again, there is here no more a reporting of war than before there had been a reporting of sorcery. The element 'from life', in the *Disasters* as in the *Caprichos*, is indeed slight; if this is not so, why write 'I have seen it myself' beneath one of the plates? Like all artists Goya eagerly probed reality for what he needed; a gesture, a kind of lighting, very often an expression; and he had discovered the gesture and the expression by isolating them from their surroundings and by introducing them into his dream, the dream to which they had given shape. The scenes in the *Disasters* play the same part. Seen, they set his memory working; told, his imagination; but he was striving after their expression and not their reconstitution and many of them seem to glide over his copper-plates like lowering clouds. The cavalry charge, for instance, the women dragged off to be raped, the corpse being pulled along, the figures fleeing before the fire, the fall of bodies under a bombardment, the monks and pillaging soldiers running, the *Riot* and even the admirable *Nada*, though that is a picture of Death. He also engraved motionless subjects; men shot, hanged or garrotted, starving beggars, the woman keeping vigil beside the dead, and the hopeless figure who, as his day of disasters fades, seems like the last living soul on earth. But this plate is no more a spectacle than is *Nada* and its essence springs from the same source. To depict an execution he draws only the victim and the levelled muskets, cut off by the margin; his beggars stand alone before an empty sky; a mass of straight lines that does not pretend to represent anything makes of his three hanged men an endless row.

The accent of the drawings for the *Disasters* is more feverish than that of the drawings for the *Caprichos*, and often Goya appears to be trying to find in them the light colour which he once took from Italy and which now gives some of the plates the appearance of states (as some of his canvases have the appearance of sketches). But all these drawings belong to the same art. Only the theatre has disappeared. There is nothing left of the stage, and no more than before is there anything of the outside world, of 'nature'. Frantic or petrified, his groups stand out against a background which is nearly always abstract. Indistinct ruins and scanty trees with lopped branches scarcely break, in the copper-plate, the white or the black which do not so much suggest sunshine or night, both equally implacable, as they recall the backgrounds of many portraits, backgrounds so intricate that they only help to emphasize the figure.

Movement now plays an important part. Goya had been familiar with the movement of witches flying through the night, of monsters who stretched out their limbs as they fell, but he is no longer concerned with the motions of limbs that fly out from crushed figures; the octopus no longer spreads out its tentacles, it entwines them together. It is not a matter of composition in the Italian sense of the word. The scene is not elaborated, it is only rarely altered; it rises up, inextricable, like a knot. This is noticeable also in the few brush drawings which were not engraved. In them Goya leaves the formalized or disjointed drawing of the *Caprichos* so far behind that he achieves a style of startling fullness, sometimes of a solidity associated with barbaric low relief. He devised a thick line which was not an arabesque but more akin in spirit to rough modelling in clay than to Tiepolo. He could not transfer the power of these sketches to his aquatints because etching would detach the figures from the background with which they formed one powerful entity; but in engraving (and in painting) he found the equivalent of this novel density in the agglomeration, hesitant at first, of secondary characters, and in experimenting with the geometric splashes of colour provided by the half-French, half-fictitious uniforms of his soldiers.

With the tapestries forgotten, and the Duke of Osuña's Alameda finished, he had lived, like many of his contemporaries, by painting portraits. The link between his work as a portrait-painter and his fictional world is the more involved because the dates of his pictures are often uncertain. But the last scenes of San Fernando – the *Triumph of the Sardine*, the *Flagellants*, and the *Madmen* belonged like their later versions to the world of the *Caprichos*. To that world belong also the *Majas on a Balcony*, painted about 1800, and the *Nude Maja* where the art is that of the portrait but the spirit is not. For that matter, almost all his great portraits of women belong in spirit to fiction.

*

GOYA: *King Charles IV of Spain with his family.* Madrid, Prado

GOYA: *Majas on a Balcony*. New York, Metropolitan Museum

GOYA: *Doña Antonia Zarate.*
New York, Miss Howard B. George

We must not forget that he painted many portraits of all kinds. In accordance with the widespread practice of the time he asked a higher price when he painted the hands. The description 'a portrait such as he alone knew how to paint, *when he wanted to'* has been applied to some, and the Bayonne *Duke of Osuña* shows us how he painted when he did not want to. Sometimes he scamped the work; sometimes he sought for colour combinations of a most exceptional quality; sometimes he worked from a model, in the *Isabel de Porcel* for instance; often he made his work part of a private world which can be recognized when a dozen of his portraits are brought together. His reputation for cruelty rests entirely on the pictures of the royal family. Now the great have no liking for seeing themselves made ugly, not even from love of good painting, and he painted the queen at least twenty times and the king fifteen. Some have expressed surprise that the family of Charles IV should have looked with pleasure on the row of Aunt Sally figures that represent it. But was not the family itself still odder, and did it not see in this frightful canvas a friendly mirror? 'She has her heart and her story in her face,' said Napoleon of the queen, 'it surpasses everything you can imagine . . .' And the questionable cruelty of Goya disappeared with the crown. Let us imagine the actual looks of his wife Josefa Bayeu, of the Condessa del Carpio, of the Tirana, of the Lady with the Fan, and of Antonia Zarate, and take each one out of her picture. We notice that there she is set off by a juxtaposition of greys, reds, and blacks, by materials with a pearly sheen, by an atmosphere of colour of a quality that belongs not to her but to Goya, colour which is in the same class as poetry. Goya idealizes *by means of colour*, as Velazquez did, and in *Charles III with his Dog* he borrows this idealization from Velazquez. In certain of the latter's thick-lipped Infantas there is a nobility which their formal pose is quite inadequate to explain. Rembrandt had already shown that a face could be ennobled as much by a particular combination of colours as by the re-alignment of the features. Goya does not attempt to ennoble; in this field he is as far from Rembrandt as Rembrandt is from Leonardo; but he aims for a metamorphosis no less complete. Unfortunately this metamorphosis does not stand up to reproduction in black and white. The passionate exertion with which he tried to tear the figures in his etchings away from their human state is met with again here, less visible but no less effective. The women he painted must have felt, much more strongly than we who can never see them, that Goya, without using empty decoration or altering their features, had gently transported them into some indefinable fairyland.

*

At this period it appears that his portraits and his imaginative works formed two groups (as El Greco's had before) though the border line may be indistinct. Which of his portraits can be put beside the *Madmen*, the *Cannibals*, or the later *Third of May, 1808*? What scene beside the *Isabel de Porcel*, *Antonia Zarate*, or the probable *Josefa Bayeu*? The two sides of his work came together later . . .

Before his illness he had painted portraits (some very beautiful) and tapestry cartoons in series (some very successful). Afterwards, he had painted, and considered very important, some scenes which broke with all the artistic standards of his own age and of many others too; who before him had painted madmen? When he became more and more sought after as a portrait-painter he had almost given up painting scenes but had engraved many; now he painted them one after the other, all closely linked together like his sets of aquatints; making up a world. As a portrait painter his art had developed into one of the richest and subtlest the West has ever known. Now, suddenly and without reason, he forgot it. The *Third of May, 1808* is not another 'group' but a *Disaster* of genius. The style of the small pictures of the war, minor works when compared with *Third of May, 1808,* is nearly always (except in the geometry of the *Monk)* much more timid than that of the *Disasters*. Compare the scenes of rape in the aquatints with those in the pictures! It could be said that these minor pictures, far from freeing him from illustration, bring him near to it. And what does their colouring owe to that of his portraits?

The portraits had to take account of their sitters, more or less, and often very much. And each sitter was unique. But these scenes, like those of the tapestries and the

GOYA: *Doña Isabel Cobos de Porcel.*
London, National Gallery

99

GOYA: *Supposed Portrait of Josefa Bayeu, the painter's wife.* Madrid, Prado

GOYA: *Lady with a Fan*. Paris, Louvre

GOYA: *Doña Maria Josefa, sister of King Charles IV*. Madrid, Prado

GOYA: Drawing without title. Madrid, Prado

engravings, belong to 'sets'. In a similar way to the subjects of Hogarth, those of Goya call for others. Even so (except in the *Maragotos)* he is not telling a story. He is striving after a confused kind of symphony; that is where his pictures, which do not follow one another, are so unlike the cycles of the Venetians. But these are not recollections any more than the *Disasters*. They are the sudden embodiments, by way of reverie and perhaps of some lingering spectacles, of an obsession to which recollection only gave its outline. If he caught a glimpse of scenes of rape, and we do not know that he did, did he see the *Brigands*? Did he see the *Human Sacrifice*? Or the murder of the Archbishop of Quebec by the *Cannibals*? But it is impossible for us not to recognize that all these pictures belong to the same world. He had undoubtedly seen the *Madmen*; but before seeing them for the first time he had waited until he was forty-seven and in poor health.

The depicting of the imaginary appealed to him because for him it represented the out-cropping of another world and not, as it had meant to Venice, Rome, and France, the embellishment of our world. His scenes of war are certainly the results of vision, but not in the sense that the word bears in painting; they are apparitions; apparitions of intercepted phantasy, like the scenes of the Inquisition and like so

GOYA: *Episode from the War of Independence.* Formerly Munich, J. Böhler

many of his aquatints. If the artist goes to the devil by way of his dreams, in time the devil comes to him, and makes his mark; but the dreams do not stop for all that.

The subjects represented are less episodes of war than it has been customary to assert, perhaps on account of their first owner, the Marquis de la Romana, the guerilla leader; most of them (even the *Execution*) depict not soldiers but brigands. The *Sacrifice* and the *Cannibals* belong to an art which culminates in the *Scourge*; so do the *Fire*, the *Plague* and the *Shipwreck*. So, in its way, does the *Exorcism*. What these quite small canvases bring to Goya's art is a lighting as individual in painting as that of the better *Caprichos* had been in engraving, and in particular the dramatic use of light. Of course, many of his pictures represent caves and the rude arrival of day through some opening. But the effect sought is the same when, instead of using an opening which hurls the light into the gloom, he has to make use of a fire; it is the same when, in the *Monk*, he uses a courtyard; the same again when, in the *Cannibals*, the source of light is twofold. In the *Plague* the choice of a prison yard allows him to place the source in the centre, like a setting sun. In these canvases, and in those they gave rise to, Goya seems to me, far from staging scenes of homicide, to be setting down a shadow that he has to people. The inhabitant of this

105

GOYA: *The Cannibals*. Besançon, Museum

oppressive cavern is misfortune. Sometimes it is murder, sometimes disaster, sometimes calamity; exceptionally, figures in costume. Without this shadow his painting is not less rich but it is no longer the same sort of painting. And when as in the *Carpet Factory*, the shadow remains but the misfortune disappears, the result is intriguing. What he is searching for now is something of which he had surmised the possibility in his later cartoons – a style of painting in which the figures, without lacking body, form an integral part of the background. His planes no longer recede by gradations; his distance becomes a luminous patch of colour. A thick background enfolds his figures instead of making them stand out; through colour combinations as 'irrational' as some sequences of musical chords it imposes the atmosphere, *not of spectacle but of the picture*, which makes Goya one of the greatest of poets. The *Greasy Pole* of the cartoon was a frolic, that of the picture is a tale of phantasy. The canvases which preserve the memory of the backgrounds of the tapestries (the *Casting of Bullets* for instance) are not among the better ones, and the admirable *Triumph of the Sardine* would be still more compact without its decorative trees. In the first *Attack on the Coach* Goya is representing, in the second, suggesting; and as for the figures swallowed up by their background, they are bringing nearer the style of the *House of the Deaf Man*. He had discovered that the

106

exact representation of a subject is not the most effective way of expressing its meaning; just as the romantics were about to do, his spirit laden with stories, symbols, and obsessions was about to rediscover poetry.

The same light would illumine the *Third of May*; but there only the victims find their style, for the monumental appearance of the soldiers removes this famous composition far away from the freedom of line to be seen in the smaller scenes and from the lyricism of a light so overpowering that in the massed shadows of some of his works the characters became indiscernible. All doubt is dispelled this time; it is plain that we have here not simply the actuality of war but its poetry.

Is it often given to an artist to embody his age-long obsessions in the suffering of a people? His art, till then incurably solitary, suddenly embodied the brotherhood of Spain. It was a complicated kind of brotherhood. Goya, like most of the liberals in his country and in the rest of Europe, had been a collaborator, though a rather passive one, and more from feelings of nobility than from interest. He had begun by looking on the French as the defenders of freedom. His protector Jovellanos had

GOYA: *The Exorcism*. Madrid, Prado

GOYA: *The first Attack on the Coach*. Madrid, Marquesa de Montellano

GOYA: *The second Attack on the Coach*. Madrid, Marquis de Castro Serna

GOYA: *'It is a hard thing.'* Etching. (Disasters 31)

been killed for serving them; and Goya was now sixty years old. The *Disasters* take on their full meaning when we realize that they are not only the work of a bitter patriot but also of a deceived friend, the sketch-book of a communist after the occupation of his country by Russian troops. When French friendship became tyranny he found himself bound to his former enemies. It was with insurgent Spain that he felt himself at one, not with the future victors; of enslaved Spain he had known only its suffering.

But when what he is depicting belongs to the horrible – seen, described to him, or imagined – then he preserves the link between it and the timeless. The man impaled, the man whose severed arms hang from the branches, figures which evoke age-old tortures and the passage, in the pages of the Bible, of the armies of Assyria, these are naked – outside time. The uniforms of his French soldiers are barely French; what fascinates him is not the courage of Spanish patriots, but the blinded, the mutilated, the tortured; the indictment of God. Bosch introduced men into his infernal world; Goya introduced the infernal into the world of man. With Bosch it is the devils who are cruel. Both their peoples are peoples of victims, but Goya knew that that was not all; they are peoples of men as well, torturers in their turn.

GOYA: '*Nothing. He will say it himself.*' Etching. (Disasters 69)

Without question he is the only painter whose message in a time of war was neither intrusive nor mocking; and he is our greatest poet of blood. I have said elsewhere that for an agnostic a possible definition of the devil is that which in man aims to destroy him. This is the devil which fascinated Goya. Satan for him is not the personage seated on Bosch's throne but a dying man whose limbs have been cut off and of whom he asks, 'Why?'

The rationalization of the religious emotion, once it had lost the accent of battle, had cut art off from its subterranean world. Voltaire believed that he had answered Pascal, but he had answered those who were 'utilizing' Pascal, forgetting that the roots of this stricken tree were indestructibly buried in the depths of the earth. The eternal question, 'What is the meaning of life *since* man is mortal?' had for centuries only been answered in Christian terms. The rationalist agnosticism of the time either passed it over or believed it had stifled it; the Bible it regarded as merely suspect history, or else it endeavoured, with Rousseau, to make love into the means of justice, forgetting that the love preached on the Mount belonged not to the heart but to the soul, was not sentimental but metaphysical, and that if it had spread over Europe this was not because it aimed to reconcile men but rather to snatch them

113

GOYA: '*Great Prowess. With dead men.*' Etching. (Disasters 39)

from a world sated with death. It was against metaphysical death, beginning with
its peremptory manifestation, cruelty, that Goya's reply was aimed. Deaf as he was,
he could always hear the voice that never fails. He knew that it knows no answer,
but he learnt that there exists between it and art the same dialogue, majestic and
hopeless, that exists between it and love.

His debt to the Christianity of the eighteenth century is contained in the idea that
politics was just adopting from the Gospels: the conviction that man has a *right* to
justice. Such a statement would seem utterly conceited to a Roman, who would
doubtless have looked upon the *Disasters* as we look upon photographs of the amphi-
theatre . . . But if Goya thought that man has not come onto the earth to be cut in
pieces he thought that he must have come there for something. Is it to live in joy
and honour? Not only that; it is to come to terms with the world. And the message
he never ceased to preach, a message underlined by war, is that man only comes
to terms with the world by blinding himself with childishness.

Goya's art had been a decoration. For two hundred years art was decoration;
sometimes admirable, and revealing individual styles. But neither the Piazza San
Marco, nor Poussin's trophies, nor the Florentine revival's hymn to joy had con-

fronted the irremediable. That had never appeared except in lightning flashes; Rembrandt and the later Hals had found again the voice of Christianity. But almost all their century, and then all the eighteenth, had preserved an invisible barrier between paintings and those who looked at them, and had confined their art to the recess which kept it apart from men. Such painting had followed the great art which preceded it like a story-teller following a preacher of genius. Gothic painting, Giotto, Michelangelo, the later Titian, Tintoretto, El Greco had thrust a conversation upon the spectator and had touched his soul; in all painting Velazquez had been the first dumb genius. But before his overpowering silence, what did Mengs say, or Bayeu, or even Hogarth, or Guardi, or Fragonard? Exactly what the Goya of the tapestries said – nothing. All art had lost the power to utter the voice that had seemed to justify its existence, and the reason was that till then the only art in the Western world that had spoken, and still spoke, was Christian art.

Secular painting and religious painting had never been rivals. Raphael did not regard himself as an agnostic; neither did Titian and still less Tintoretto. Louis Le Nain did not consider himself a Michelangelo, and eighteenth-century art did not range itself against the Christian masters, as modern art more or less openly does; it established itself in the gaps in their genius like the stalls under the arches of the Colosseum. At its worst it aimed at decoration; at its best, a picture. But the *Madhouse* was not only a picture; the *Third of May, 1808* is decidedly not one.

This appeal to the spectator, this desire to involve him, in and by a spectacle and even beyond the spectacle, had spread throughout Gothic art but had not re-appeared except in flashes among the great Venetians. (Afterwards there had been its lesser imitator in erotic art, that dialogue of an inferior hell.) This dialogue is not indispensable to art, although art on occasion finds in it one of its most telling effects; but it is what Goya was going to recover. In Europe it had been inseparable from the only language used by the everlasting – the language of Christ. Goya, and he was the first to do so, seems to want to draw a language from the darkness. He restored the forgotten dialogue, but with another voice.

This dialogue in which the spectator is silent often arises when painting tells him something he would have preferred not to hear; when it *compels* him to listen. The Christians of the fifteenth century believed that they ought to pay attention to the horrifying sermons, preached in charnel houses, describing the Passion and going on, hour after hour, to the verge of delirium. They believed that they ought to look at Grünewald's *Crucifixion*, but no doubt they would have looked at it even if they had not thought it sin to turn away their eyes. Man does not gaze only on what he prefers; the love that terrifies is called fascination.

The *Third of May, 1808* and some of the *Disasters* call to mind Dostoievsky's great novels. The two artists were suddenly cut off from men by the irremediable

GOYA: *The Vulture*. Preparatory Drawing. Madrid, Prado

(and the House of the Deaf Man would be a fitting habitation for the Karamazoffs
. . .). Dostoievsky's novels were, and still are, narratives; but they become a sermon,
obscurely and vehemently expressed as all modern prophecy is. What is a prophet,
if he is not a man who speaks to others in order to open their eyes, to tear them from
the world of appearances and give them the world of Truth? And the truth of a
painter is no more a doctrine than is the truth of a musician; it consists of pictures
which first make the world vulnerable and then a cheat. Gaze your fill upon madmen, but, when you have gazed on them, look at yourself in the glass! Gaze on
Goya's art, but when you have gazed on it, look at the world of men reeling. The
shock which Dostoievsky gives to our dreams springs less from the picture of the
murderer and the prostitute reading the story of Lazarus together like brother and
sister, than from the fact that it consigns to incurable emptiness so many pitiful
readings under all the lamps burning in the Russian night . . .

Perhaps one could define romanticism as an attempt to recover the irrational or
superhuman world that man and Christianity had lost between them, and for which
Christian terms no longer provided the artistic expression; there can be no doubt
that one could so define Goya, to whom that domain beckoned for many painful

GOYA: *The Vulture*. Etching. (Disasters 76)

reasons. At that time the irremediable could not express itself without destroying the harmony that it found before it. Such emotion in a Christian artist had been able to give birth to Grünewald's work but it seemed fated in Europe to nothing but a silent and lonely death. Until the war came Goya's message had been hesitant. Justified by the horrible in a world whose Christianity was now nothing but a decoration, it crushed that decoration in the same way as the first great Christian sculptors rejected the art of antiquity. Like them, Goya meant to find again the sacred language.

For him it was the dialogue with fate, and the words on which he drew were those of the Devil; to his dreamer's eyes the sacred, which had never been the Church, was no longer even the divine.

A great artist does not depict horror for the sake of horror, any more than he depicts battles for the sake of battles or still life for the sake of still life. The Christian artist sees in it an adjuration; no voice more readily brings home to man a realization of his condition: but becoming redemptive, it brings together the host that cannot reach God unless swept along by the angel of terror. But to what God does Goya's horror lead?

GOYA: Brush drawing without title. Madrid, Prado

Perhaps in the first place to Goya himself. The artist affected by the irremediable often tries to people his loneliness, 'Hypocrite lecteur, mon semblable, mon frère . . .' Infirmity is less terrible when absurdity is universal, deafness less grievous in the midst of corpses, and perhaps Goya found a kind of brotherhood among the tormented bodies he engraved; he calls God to account by means of these appalling proxies.

The artist's struggle against a god in whom he does not believe would be unthinkable did it not dimly express the very old idea that the creator is not the true God. In India God is primarily the absolute, not the creator. Once deity and creation are separated, equilibrium can be re-established by handing the world over to the Devil. Such a view can easily be rationalized, much more so than making society into the Devil and nature into the manifestation of God as so many ideologists of Goya's time were doing. But then the creator is still the creator, and perhaps the master after death, and there is no proof that the true God cares about mankind. The metaphysical absurdity remains untouched, embellished merely, for the accuser of a creator who is of the devil but may be all-powerful, by the illusion of moments of frantic heroism. The artist can only come to terms with fate (this was the Italian style), ignore it (the style of eighteenth-century France), or indict it. Goya did not

116

come to terms with it, nor did he ignore it. It is not less in the nature of man to want to be immortal than to know that he is man.

Goya was, no doubt, acquainted with those moments in Spanish art when hope seems dead and Christ nothing but a tortured figure. But he knew that if Christ is not the very meaning of the world, then the body of an executed felon by the roadside is more significant than a crucifix. It has been said that he began the depicting of tortures, but baroque piety gorged itself on them. Ribera six times depicted St. Bartholomew being flayed alive. But St. Bartholomew died to bear witness and Goya writes beneath one of his most harrowing victims: 'For having been born in another country'. Christian art was an answer; his art is a question. The Mocking is a pathetic subject but not a ridiculous one because Jesus has chosen to be mocked. The garrotted victims of the Inquisition have not chosen the pointed cap that shakes in their agony; the laughter of soldiers before a tortured body is a question because the body did not choose to die.

From the day the insurrection broke out until the time when Goya finally forgot it (the soldiers in the House of the Deaf Man fire only on ghosts) his work is full of confused alternations between spectacle, recollection, and the obscure passion of which this recollection becomes sometimes the outward expression. The most profound exposition of life in prison is not given by Dostoievsky in the *Recollections of the House of the Dead* but in the *Brothers Karamazoff*. While most of the copperplates of the *Disasters* belong to 1810, some came later, and the *Third of May, 1808* was painted at the Restoration. Goya already knew how seriously the victory of the Spain he held so dear was threatened. Hence the bond that united him to the victims, but hence also the ease with which he brought the courage to which he devoted his genius into subjection to the ridiculous from which that courage had seemed to deliver him. And yet by identifying himself with the anguish of a people, his anguish has gained its weight of blood and often of austere pity. It is not long since he hesitated to leave the *Caprichos* for painting, but the puppets are growing now like spectres; they grow until they culminate in the little crucified arms of the man shot in the *Third of May, 1808*.

To the demand for harmony, romanticism was soon to oppose dream or epic. Goya opposed both to it. His Men facing the Firing Squad, seen by Michelangelo, would present a very different aspect from his witches. The old word masterpiece comes to mind, more compellingly perhaps than with any other of Goya's pictures; and yet it is this picture which killed the then accepted idea of a masterpiece and separated genius from the ornate world to which it was bound. Perhaps Goya had a premonition that it had been painted, for all posterity, to confront the *Coronation of Napoleon* . . . It belongs to the realm of obsession; many plates from the *Disasters – With or without Reason*, for example, and *No Remedy* – had prepared the way for it or followed it. All kinds of pictures about shootings had

GOYA: *The Third of May, 1808.* Preparatory Drawing. Pierre Jeannerat Collection

GOYA: *The Third of May, 1808: Execution of Rebels.* Madrid, Prado

GOYA: *The Second of May, 1808: The Skirmish at Puerta del Sol.* Oil sketch. Private Collection

called it forth. It is, from the opposite angle, Tolstoy's famous scene where the wounded Prince Andrew looks at the clouds ceaselessly drifting over the anguish of his companions at Austerlitz. Here, the absurdity of being man is for once vanquished and can henceforward only make a murmuring like the sea to accompany the cry of a hero without a name.

The agreement was short-lived. Feelings of brotherhood fertilized Goya's art, they did not set limits to it. His genius sprang from other sources; from the dialogue that has gone on, ever since the songs of Sumeria, between the closed lips of a tortured child and the face, for ages past invisible – and perhaps inexorable – of God. He also bears witness, on the other side. An endless procession of misery moves forward from the depth of ages towards these figures of horror and accompanies their torments with its subterranean chorus. Beyond the tragedy to his country this man who heard no longer wished to lend his voice to the deep silence of death. The war was over, but not absurdity.

GOYA: '*No one knows wherefore.*' Etching. (Disasters 36)

'DON'T WAKEN THEM'

THE victors forgave Goya because of his talent, he regarded them as profiteers from the struggle against invasion and did not forgive their ridiculous forgiveness. He painted their portraits in bitterness, and in a 'restored' Madrid lined up the ghosts of those who had died there in vain; then he painted that *Session of the Philippine Council* whose empty space waits for the coffin of Spain. He took refuge in the *Tauromachia* and etched new *Disasters*. Once again he was waiting for his short-lived Justice, seeing it appear and disappear; 'Divine reason, leave not one of them!' They had already come back.

He now knew everything that he could extract from the spectacle of suffering. The feeling of subjection that he was experiencing more and more – he was now seventy – was about to find a new embodiment, the dungeon of the Inquisition. He had already depicted it occasionally, the trials and punishments before its tribunal had figured as a dramatic carnival. But now he found again in the people of the dungeons the people he had found in the struggle against the French – the victims of all his enemies. He still depicts the unfortunate, but the illustrious are also among the convicted. The imposture which ever afterwards obsessed him was that which made injustice certain. Just as when he was confronted by war, his fierce compassion is like a feeling of brotherhood which has been cooped up. He does not so much pity the victims as feel that he is one of them. The state of mankind is also a prison and the people in it that he loathes first are the traffickers in hope. Before politicians and doctors he was content to sneer; if monks obsess him it is because they are impostors in the name of Christ.

Is he anti-Christian? Not more than he was some while before. His satirizing of monks kept up a tradition of Catholicism; when they fought the French he felt reconciled with them. He does not like priests but he is fond of the charitable orders. The religious works of his youth were of secondary importance; neither the *St. Joseph of Calasanz* nor the *Agony in the Garden* would be that. But Christianity requires faith and he had none. His Christ is not an enemy, nor yet the Son of God. He is within a metaphysical world (just as he is a prophet within Islam) which he does not transcend. This world is often the Christian world without Grace, a world whose redeemer has not yet come or where he cannot come. And sometimes life itself – his own to begin with – seemed to Goya a deception practised by God.

He had written beneath a scene of execution, 'One cannot look at this'; during the war he drew what one could not look at – the condemnation of a legless cripple, men in chains, the 'For getting married in their own way', the widow, the terror-

GOYA: *A Prisoner*. Preparatory Drawing. Madrid, Prado

124

GOYA: *A Prisoner*. Etching, reversed. (Disasters 85)

stricken. He drew these for himself; the *Prisoners* were unknown (and the *Disasters* unpublished) till after his death. Some captions take on a comforting tone; for the wretched women fallen asleep at last he revives, without knowing it, the words of Michelangelo's *Night* in the famous epigram—'*Don't waken us*!' But his work could only be an indictment. He had forgotten the traditional means of expression. The arms of the man shot in the *Third of May* do not hang down, they are stretched upward; like a modern novelist he knew that laughter can express the anguish of a condemned man better than tears; he did not symbolize, he exposed, using a broken, breathless, manner which made all the drawing of his time seem decoration.

He had learnt much, in particular all the methods of using light, from the most rational, such as the beam that illumines the significant object (the cripple's crutches), to the least rational, such as a calling in of shadow rather like the introduction of low tones in music. Going beyond the harsh curves of certain drawings in the *Disasters*, the style of the *Caprichos* returns in greater strength; the line no longer recalls a broken reed but a fractured stone; before long, a little less angular, it would herald Daumier.

This style was added to others, it did not replace them. His genius once revealed he had not, after 1800, returned to his style of pompons and mantillas. But one of the styles of the *Caprichos*, and those of the *Disasters*, persisted in his brush-drawings. Most of these, executed for his own amusement or like a writer taking notes, are of a few figures, or single ones; in such cases his style allies itself to the *Caprichos*. The designs of the 'compositions' are no longer gratuitous, and we instinctively class them among the preparatory sketches to the *Disasters*, the *Tauromachia*, or the *Disparates*, for his design cannot give full scope to its function except when it has none, that is to say, when it depicts a single figure. Certain drawings containing several figures, drawings in which light and concentrated colour play an important part and which cannot be classed in sequences, seem to be on the way to becoming pictures. I do not believe that they are 'studies' but rather that Goya, who followed his obsessions, 'let them come'; the drawing of *Saturn* is one of Goya's moments of obsession, not a study for the House of the Deaf Man.

GOYA: '*A pretty couple.*' Drawing. Madrid, Prado

126

GOYA: *Mutual Help*. Drawing. Madrid, Prado

His important drawings, moreover, carry in almost every case the mark of recollection. None of them is evidence that he had spent his life making sketches in prison cells. He was permanently on the look-out for shapes but he was not subservient to them. Selection was called in – by his feeling. What he saw only clarified the indistinct accusing shapes that he carried within him. Let us only remember the cry of Daumier, who to all appearances found sketching so simple: 'You know perfectly well that I cannot draw from nature!'

He began the *Disparates*, that is, the Madnesses; feminine madness, matrimonial madness, the madness of poverty and of carnival, flying madness, common madness, the madness of fright, raging madness, sheer madness, and the *Old Man straying among Phantoms*. There is no more comedy and old women with mirrors but majestic apparitions, the spectre of War, murder, monsters, men sewn up in sacks, and the figure with three legs and two heads symbolizing marriage and perhaps love. Undoubtedly Goya has shown himself in these works to be the greatest interpreter of anguish the West has ever known. Once his genius had hit upon the deep melody of the song of Evil it mattered little whether in the depths of the night his multitudes of shades, his throng of owls and witches, returned to haunt him or not.

This art has been called a popular art, a judgement which seems fair and yet at the same time odd. A painter does not become identified with the people for having painted a knife-grinder, a woman carrying water, blacksmiths, insurgents, three-hundred portraits of aristocrats, and eighty-eight pictures of the royal family. The people of Spain were his brothers, especially during the struggle for independence, but the popular element in Goya is to be found less in his subjects, his art, or his friendships, than in his brotherhood with phantoms. Dwarfs belong to the Middle Ages, and to undying legend. Like Shakespeare, Goya remained in tune with the world of legend from which the great romantics would keep merely the picturesque, an aspect known only to the people at that time, and the source whence *Macbeth* had taken its Homeric ring.

Gobineau, on a journey to Persia, disembarked by night at the port of Malta. In that town, where golden saints have fibre on their heads instead of white hair because the sacristans grow lentils in their crowns, he met a Harlequin playing a guitar before the closed windows of an hotel taken from that imaginary Mediterranean of which Molière was dreaming in the *Sicilian*; next, a black cat between the still standing Venetian houses, to the strains and the glitter of opera; then a band of musketeers and the entire cast of the Italian comedy singing as they entered. The confetti at last forced him to recall what the crossing had put out of his mind – he had arrived on a night of carnival . . . Goya's carnival is not entirely invention; like that which dazzled Gobineau, like that of great poets, of children's games, or of the oldest dreams, it is another world. His figures are not people in fancy dress,

Goya: *Saturn*. Drawing. Madrid, Prado

129

TIEPOLO: *Carnival Scene.* Paris, Louvre

they are butterflies hatched out for a fleeting moment from a larval world, the Revelation of freedom. 'I would like to be that gentleman going past!', says Fantasio, who above all wanted to be Harlequin. The most wretched fancy-dress figure wants to be, for one night at least, someone else; the medieval Mardi Gras had been the epic of irresponsibility. This carnival is not only the dream made less wild; it is also the call of man set free to the unknown world which his deliverance desires. But Goya did not play at fairy-tale castles; for him the supernatural meant first of all an illumination which he spread over his masks as Rembrandt hurled down his light over his figures of pity. To understand its language it is perhaps sufficient to compare the throng of his fancy-dress characters with the masqueraders of Tiepolo.

His work goes beyond the fairy-land of Venice, as it goes beyond the decorative effects of galleys . . . His unconquerable dreams, *Saturn*, the *Pilgrimage to San Isidro* (even the *Third of May* which belongs to them and whose sky is theirs), owe no more to this spirit than they do to the organizers of spectacles mentioned in Latin orators, but they do have an affinity with the curse-tormented characters in Aeschylus. His Fates, for the first time, obscurely recall the tones of the Eumenides. His imagination scarcely invents, rather it revives in anguish shapes lost in the

GOYA: *The Burial of the Sardine*. Madrid, Academy of San Fernando

darkness of Genesis. Certain of his compositions look like the work of a medium; there are some, such as the *Dog's Head* of the House of the Deaf Man, and several *Disparates*, of which we search for the meaning; there are others where we scarcely make out what they represent.

One of his most important canvases, the *Burial of the Sardine*, represents Ash Wednesday, the obsequies of carnival, the death of the time during which men believed they were free and were glad because they were forgetting that they had just borne the features of the dead. He engraved a world turned upside-down, in other words the Saturnalia; the donkey, the he-goat, the monkey, the cat, the bat, the crippled, the mad, the hanged, the man-skeleton, men-chickens, men sawn in two, flagellants, the tribunals of the Inquisition, nightmares, flying men and bulls, brigands, rapes, tortures, the stake, murders, executions, abandoned children, human sacrifice, cannibals; foetuses, gnomes, giants and dwarfs, sorcerers, devils, spectres, the Fates; prostitution, prisons, famine, shipwreck, fire, plague. Is this Spain? What other Spaniard has painted it? Yet who has touched with equal

sureness the blind monsters of age-old depths, the symbols buried for thousands of years beneath our memory? Once the tapestries were finished, the portraits and religious scenes put aside, he did not paint ten spectacles that do not belong to a troubled world, from prostitution to torture. His mythological characters, his *Psyche*, seem to be another's work. Like the eyes of a cat, his imagination only lights up in the dark. When he allegorizes his country he spreads over it the wings of Time. He had painted the Commander; if he paints Hercules it is at Omphale's side; if Biblical characters, he chooses Susanna and especially Judith; his sexuality is never far from blood. The Judith on his wall was not enough for him, he

GOYA: *Cupid and Psyche*.
Barcelona, Cambó Collection

133

GOYA: Drawing without title. Madrid, Prado

repeated it with a figure of slaughter. At last, Saturn . . . We have, at one and the same time, the other world and our world suddenly grown fertile, our world by night, lit by the gleam of a dead star and carrying, in the implacable orbit of the planets, its throbbing dreams whose beat is as deaf, as old, and as unconquerable as the beating of the heart of man. Goya's genius moved now in a world of correspondences where the thin strains of a living man summoned up the deep orchestra of the immemorial past.

His shapes become confused, or allusive. The conical hat of the Inquisition is that of the wizard. St. Isidore appears to the king like a great dragon-fly. The man with padlocks for ears is no collage. What disturbs us in the flying men is first the contradiction between the plate's background, its black at once that of aquatint, of darkness, and of the abstract (the black of the *Caprichos*), and the depth conferred

GOYA: *The Dog.* (House of the Deaf Man.) Madrid, Prado

135

by the small dimensions of the distant figures; but there is also the disagreement between the parachute cords stretched tight by the exertions of the chief character, and the small figure above that character's head. Looked at from right to left beginning with the eye it is the head of a bird of prey; looked at from left to right it is something else. It appears again, in outline, in the flying man below, and makes the outstretched wings suggest Satan. How many of Goya's pictures stretch out in time or mystery, as though they were only the imprint left by the passage of the supernatural! He was so well aware of this prolonging that he readily painted them in pairs; the *Nude Maja* and the clothed, the *Second* and *Third of May*, the *Old Women* and the *Young Women (Majas Out Walking)*. His instinct guided him to every form of suggestion that he employed; the suggestion of shadow, of red and black (blood and darkness), of the dull greens in the small, ghastly pale pictures painted at the end of his life, of the design which joins the face to mask or animal, of the composition which cuts off the rifles so that the firers do not appear. In the foreground of the *Mason* the stone opposite to the workman's broken leg is split in two, the soldiers of the *Third of May* are turned into a prophetic throng, and the arms of the executed into those of Christ. The mystery of the vertical rock that the figures in the *Vision* point to, as of that in the *Fantastic Landscape*, is the mystery of the life in the houses that rise above them, for these seem to be inaccessible. The extension beyond the picture of the scene represented, to which some of the *Caprichos* had owed their power of suggestion, now reappears in a greater degree. 'Where's Mother going?' asks a voice when the witch flies away. Bystanders gaze idly on his scenes of the marvellous, soldiers fire on his flying figures; the fantastic is strengthened by the innocent spectators that it astonishes, it annexes a world that it renders surrealistic – the world of the *Giant's* country, and of *Saturn's* limbs which are also storm clouds. The lance of the madman in the *Disparates* is thrust through the eye of a severed head (not found in the preliminary sketch). Compare *The Madness of Fear* with the *Bogey-man* of the *Caprichos*!

What did he paint on the walls of his house? In the dining-room, a woman beside a bed, an old man, Saturn, Judith, a pilgrimage, a witches' sabbath; on the first floor, men eating, a dog looking up appealingly, Fates, two men fighting with cudgels, laughing women, two flying figures, a monk, and a scene of people reading. Six fantastic or fabulous scenes and six scenes of 'realism'? But the bed behind the woman is eroticism; the figure behind the patriarch is death; the eaters are themselves death. As early as the *Christ taken Prisoner* of Toledo he had suggested the subject by the expression on the face of one of the tormentors. The fighting shepherds and the dog sink into the ground; and the Pilgrims are going to the Sabbath from which the laughing women seem to have slipped away. Here, the very idea of realism no longer has any meaning. If we assume that there were models for these women, for the monk, or for the eaters, we should have to assume that Goya is

GOYA: *Procession of Flagellants*. Madrid, Academy of San Fernando

GOYA: *Judith.* (House of the Deaf Man.) Madrid, Prado

GOYA: *Judith*. Drawing. Madrid, Prado

GOYA: *One Way of Flying*. Etching. (Disparates 13)

recalling an expression he has glimpsed, and that expression would be the fleeting traces on a human face of the world revealed in his Fates suspended in the air and in his flying figures; levitation is a very old dream, to be found in the witches' broomstick and the magic carpet of the East.

The change that began with the first *Caprichos* had now plumbed all its depths. No artist, not even Baudelaire, has revealed so clearly the power of the irremediable. Goya wanted the world to admit that it was only an appearance, a deception per- haps; he expressed it by a colouring which denies its colouring. The 'dark paintings' of the House of the Deaf Man obviously do not possess the glowing colours of the pictures which are contemporary with them; but the latter deny reality as much as the former, which call them forth – and are inseparable from them. So as to destroy not only this reality but also the style through which it claimed to be glorified Goya made use of the system of correspondences and allusions that we have seen, and turned into discords every one of the essential harmonies on which the ordering of the world was based. The world was nothing but a dictionary from which he chose words simply for the hints their richness gave of times earlier than history. It has been said that he was dreaming; rather, he was excavating. The supremacy of this art is undoubtedly due to the ease with which he moves in the lost domain where we think we discern the source of our bondage. For the first time (in how many

GOYA: *Raging Madness*. Detail from an etching. (Disparates 6)

centuries!) an artist heard welling up inside himself a message which was nothing but the never-ending song of darkness. The 'dark paintings' belong to the great *Disparates*.

The subtlest of these, *Strange Madness*, plays on the precariousness of life, suggested by the branch of a dead tree, on the cadaveric face of one of the women, on the owl's face of another, on the group's resemblance to a nest of night birds, on the strangeness of the meeting, of the garrulous hand, and of the check pattern of the shawl, and lastly on sleep and night with the pallid dash of colour below that hints at the moon ... Let us not forget the part played in story by the hand – where fate is written – and by the birds of night, which symbolize or accompany the Devil. The *Family of Charles IV* would be less disturbing if the face of the Queen did not rise above it like an owl's head.

Hitherto the drawing which went beyond a sketch had been the study for a picture if it was not a study for a line-engraving; when it was a study for an etching it

GOYA: '*Everyone will fall.*' Etching. (Capricho 19)

GOYA: *Strange Madness.* Etching. (Disparates 3)

143

GOYA: *'Here's the Bogey-man.'* Etching. (Caprichos 3)

GOYA: *Madness of Fear*. Etching. (Disparates 2)

tended to become independent. It prepared the way to the etching which led the way to another – something which the picture had never done to the same extent because it was in colour. (This sequence is already visible in Rembrandt, although his drawing is less closely allied to engraving). Into the closed world of the etching colour does not enter again except by force. Accustomed to a technique where colour is expressed only by black and white, the painter is led to employ colour, like black and white, to express and not to represent. Is it the etching technique which relates some of Goya's pictures to those of Rembrandt rather than to Hals, even though his strokes and colouring are much nearer to the latter than to the former? Without etching, the House of the Deaf Man would be more of a mystery; the reproduction of the *Old Man straying among Phantoms* seems to belong to it; engraving has become painting.

*

GOYA: *The Old Man straying among Phantoms.* Etching. (Disparates 18)

Protected by the bodyguard of mummers and phantoms with which he had covered his walls he broke off his harsh converse with these swarming spectres and resumed that which, thirty years earlier, he had begun, alone, with painting and which he now pursued alone. Was he still afraid of madness? How at home it would be here! The apparitions, stealthy at first, had taken possession of the house as of Goya himself. He had granted them a life by night, something a little more substantial than the life in black and white of his engravings and fancies, a life in monochrome painting. They were growing into the murmuring that heralded the harsh majestic tones that he called his colour. If once he should attempt with colour what their dull, leaden world – suggestive of what Rembrandt's hell might have been – was attempting to do without colour, then painting would cease to be in bondage. Goya knew now that if there is a loneliness where the lonely man is rejected by his fellows, there is also another where he is lonely only because mankind has not yet come to him. He had understood why prophets find their strength in the wilderness; and his wilderness, which gave him the strength to impose his spectres, gave him also the strength to impose a language deeper than theirs, the language foreshadowed at the time of the first *Madmen*. Just as he had imposed his visions on Spain, so now he was going to impose his spirit, which was as present in certain ways of juxtaposing red and black as it was in a people of apparitions.

146

GOYA: *The Pilgrimage to the Pool of San Isidro.* (House of the Deaf Man.) Madrid, Prado

And the blinded swarming of the phantoms watched over the feverish heart-searching in which he discovered modern colouring.

At his birth the European spirit had been regarded as a system of order; when Goya died that spirit was scarcely regarded as anything. With the Renaissance art had become separate from what it expressed. It had passed from the service of religion to the service of civilization, of an ornate image that man made of himself. In the Italian-French corpus of accepted notions which had conquered Europe, the 'enlightenment' of the philosophers in no way clashed with that of the Jesuits from whom they had learnt their early lessons. The French revolutionaries revered David. All art of the time was a hierarchy.

This hierarchy Goya either rejected or ignored. It has been maintained that Spain was obsessed by it; but the etiquette of the Court, like Byzantine ceremonial, belonged to the sphere of religion. 'I am the State. – How few you are then!', the almost sacred shade of Philip II replies to the ghost of Louis XIV. Spain was regarded at the time, rightly, as an enemy of refinement; the mistake lay in deeming her barbarous, and from time to time she undertook to prove its mistake to the world.

The age worshipped French literature and English painting. The latter was born of the annexation by the aristocracy, through Van Dyck, of a part of Rubens; Titian, transplanted to England, ended in Gainsborough. Artistic quality and elegance were carefully mingled there. But English painters respected their aristocracy. What did Señor Goya, Royal Painter, think of the Court? Up to the time of Ferdinand he seems not to have felt any marked aversion for the nightmare royalties that followed one another before his eyes; rather, he was gratified to find in the

GOYA: *The Monk*. (House of the Deaf Man.) Madrid, Prado

GOYA: *King Ferdinand VII*. Madrid, Prado

149

GOYA: *The Fates*. (House of the Deaf Man.) Madrid, Prado

king the symbol of universal absurdity, a holy fool. Whatever one may say, he had painted his aristocrats without animosity (the women often with pleasure). The middle classes did not interest him except as characters for his theatre. As to the peasants and artisans he had for years made of them what most painters, writers, and musicians of the time had made of them – characters for frescoes and light operas. His special debt to the people was, as we have seen, his dreams.

He did not then fancy himself as an aristocratic painter, certainly not as a 'refined' one; it is enough to compare the Lille *Young Women (Majas Out Walking)* with Gainsborough, or with the *Signboard for Gersaint*! But compare them with a figure of Chardin and it will be obvious how little of the bourgeois was in Goya. Society mattered little to him, in an age when society was all-powerful even over the style of Fragonard and Guardi. And he was equally indifferent to the middle classes. For him, distinction was something conferred by poetry. Gainsborough's more studiously elaborate figures do not stand up well to a comparison with that of *Antonia Zarate;* so true is it that it is better to be an enchantress than a duchess. After the gorgeous red that English painters of the time used so much – partly because of uniforms – look at the red, always a little disturbing, of Goya; the red that goes so well with the black cat of little *Manuel Osorio*. Those scattered glimpses of fairy-land in his work, glimpses reserved for his women, for some men he loved, and for children, are the results merely of colour-combinations which cannot be reduced to a system. He was in no sense of the word a preacher of plebeian values; those which, without thinking too much about them, he opposed to aristocratic values, were not popular values, but artistic. His art's ideal admirer was neither Pope, king, nor people, but other artists.

150

GOYA: *The Fates*. Detail. (House of the Deaf Man.) Madrid, Prado

When he was linked with the people it was by his emotions, not by his art. I am still referring only to his representation; his inventive work reveals yet another side of his nature. His representation not only attacked social quality for the sake of artistic quality; it attacked the ordering of the world for the benefit of mystery. What form of Western art had not tried to concentrate on some divine element in man? In a century which set its heart on consciousness – and logic, even to the guillotine – Goya introduced the unconscious. Sade's garrulous characters are blanched with the pallor of the dungeon while Goya's figures bring with them the haunted night, but both have the same adversary – that 'enlightenment' that Sade and Goya thought they revered.

The man of Reason was trying to take the place of saint and hero, and Saint-Just did not regard his own world as any less coherent than the world of Louis XIV.

GOYA: *The Pilgrimage to San Isidro.* Detail. (House of the Deaf Man.) Madrid, Prado

152

GOYA: *The Pilgrimage to San Isidro*. Detail. Madrid, Prado

GOYA: *Meeting of Witches*. (House of the Deaf Man.) Madrid, Prado

David agreed with Saint-Just; with what did Goya agree? With the notion that art can win the consent of the spectator, living or to be born, by appeals *which cannot be rationalized*. For this to be proved true it was perhaps essential that the idea of man on which Europe had lived should collapse.

There was no system of man behind Goya, and perhaps this was so far the first time, for the devils of Flanders were not unaware of Christ. The dreams of Chartres were a saint's dreams, of Rome, a hero's; Goya's were the dreams of a medium. He had been delivered from the angels more by phantoms than by devils. The way was open – towards what?

His guide was the instinct that everything sacred (and that which he opposed to beauty, whether he knew it or not, was indeed sacred) rested on *awareness* of the other world, that it had been obscured by the passionate eagerness of humanity to arrange the world to suit itself. This 'sacred' which obsessed him is striking to us by reason of its negative character – a photographic negative which suggests its print, a dark glass through which the stars are plain to see. But the bond that unites

154

the dreadful with the sacred is strong in a people that for two thousand years has worshipped a man put to torture. And Greece, which in the memory of man still remains Arcadia, expressed its idea of the sacred by a god who devoured his children, by ghosts, and by a hero's torn-out eyes. The sacred whose invisible presence would not be suggested by myths, like the presence of a wind by its passage across our brows, the sacred that would not be revealed by the light which it shed on the road that led towards itself, would necessarily be inexpressible. The only means that art had of attempting this expression lay in re-establishing contact with everything which used the artist only as an intermediary – with blood, mystery, and death. It remains true that harvests are as eternal as calamity, and Cybele as Persephone; but it is equally true that an artist does not choose his contact with the sacred and that for almost all the arts the crop springs up also from the land of the dead. But the aspect of the sacred which comes to the surface or appears only by overturning the relationships established by man compelled Goya to choose moments, real or imaginary, when our relationships are overturned – games, the

GOYA: *Young Majas*. Lille, Museum

GAINSBOROUGH: *Mrs. Richard Brinsley Sheridan.* Washington, National Gallery of Art (Mellon Collection)

157

carnival, madness, the corrida, monsters, horror, tortures, and darkness. Not love, and certainly not motherhood. In the *Disasters* he drew only children snatched from their mothers, there are no women among the sobbing spectators of the *Third of May*. His patriots conquer or die almost alone; his crowds are always mere on-lookers. The only Christ of his that can grip us is in the Garden of Olives. At a pinch he painted that which brings crowds together (patriotism, but also calamity), not that which unites a few individuals. Love also forms part of the sacred, but it is its opposite pole.

Such loneliness has its limits, for Goya was not a prophet but a painter. If he had not been a painter his attitude to life would have found its expression only in preaching or suicide. But he was an artist, and that meant that his attitude could not be reduced to absurdity; however complete subjection may be, however lasting the secret seal of death, the artist does not believe in advance that they are the conquerors in the dizzy moment when man takes possession of them by imposing on them his transfiguration. Goya is not the rival of the God who allows them, because he depicts tortures but because he makes of each one of them a Promethean cry of pain in the night. Rembrandt, who tried several times to paint the *Pilgrims of Emmaus* before he produced the final canvas in the Louvre, was evidently worried about its setting. But it was not in the setting that he hoped to find his communion with the most poignant, and humbling, moment of the Resurrection, nor in the admirable face of Christ; he sought it in the indivisible whole – a whole irreducible to a representation – that is a great work of art, as Titian did in his *Pietà* of Venice, and Piero della

GOYA: *Old Man eating*. (House of the Deaf Man.) Madrid, Prado

158

GOYA: *Laughing Woman*. (House of the Deaf Man.) Madrid, Prado

Francesca in his *Adoration of the Shepherds*. The Sung landscape painter was not diverting himself when he painted the mist, he was using it to express the Buddhist communion between man and the world. The Aztec sculptor looked for a more sombre communion with the powers of darkness not from the death's head, but

GOYA: *The Old Women*. Lille, Museum

from the expression he gave to it. Painting, for Goya, was a means of achieving mystery, but at the same time mystery was for him a means of achieving painting.

His fearful testimony allowed him to engrave with genius just as his genius allowed him to testify. He had wanted to make etchings, now he wanted to produce pictures; and his art is so near to ours for this reason, that he took a spectacle and, striking as it was, submitted it to a unity *of a different kind*. Now if Goya owed his liberation from the traditional style to his pursuit of mystery, it is clear that he owed his genius only to the conquest of his personal style. This style was inconceivable without that struggle against civilization of which Goya was the harbinger; but once civilization was put in question, and the harmony of the world rejected, the function of painting began to change. It is true that the great masters had allied their genius to a method of representation sometimes, but to a system of values always. But they had at the same time pursued the strictly technical researches which made their work the expression of those values. Poussin believed in the harmony of the world, but he also believed in the connexion between yellow and blue; and especially in the ability of a particular yellow and a particular blue to express the harmony of the world. Goya believed in the transfiguring power of yellow, of grey, and of the browns in which he painted the House of the Deaf Man, but his colouring is far from being allied to mystery or the sacred in the same way that Poussin's is allied to harmony. It is not employed to make a statement of what is, but of what he is; to some degree it is used to ask a question. It is not in the service either of a rational world or of an ordered one. Rembrandt's order was of a musical type, but his world was emphatically ordered; Goya's was not, but his art is because it is an art. He can see the living through the eyes of phantoms, but the phantoms must be painters. He was not delirious and he was still a portrait painter; and he was the first artist to have a presentiment of a kind of painting which accepts no law but the law of its own unforeseeable development.

This is what our contemporaries call *Painting;* a Painting which discovers its own individual law, a law which many great painters had suspected but which none had dared to proclaim – the pre-eminence of the resources peculiar to painting over those of representation; the right to draw and paint, not to achieve an illusion or to express a spectacle in the strongest possible way, but so as to express painting itself. The anxious boldness with which Goya used green on the horse in the *Insurrection of May the Second* was now left far behind – the colours of his apparitions have no explanation but his pictures.

He did not anticipate any one of present-day artists – he foreshadowed the whole of modern art because modern art takes its rise from this freedom. He painted the *Water-Seller*, and the *Smiths* (who were at first breakers of stones). He painted the *Old Women*, a fantasy in glowing red, and the *Young Women (Majas Out Walking)* where the lacquers stand out against extraordinary areas of chalky colour. Certain canvases of that time are all the more beautiful in that they unite in themselves the successive aspects of his inspiration. The old call is still strong. The *Young Women*, the *Tio Paquete*, even the last *Majas on the Balcony* and the *Session*, are portraits. But the Tio is blind, the young women are the counterpart of the old ones who call for death; the shadows of the gallants standing behind the Majas are the shadows of devils from the *Caprichos*, and the *Session* seems to be keeping vigil over the death agony of Spain.

Over a long period, at the same time as he had been setting shape free from illusion by a treatment that was, like Manet's, neither impressionist nor expressionist – shall we say, at the same time as he had been foregoing volume, in the *There is no one to help them*, for instance – it had happened that in other figures he had sacrificed everything to it. Not to the subject's volume but to volume for its own sake, the volume of the Sumerians and certain Precolumbians, the volume which is most often linked with architecture. The soldiers in the *Third of May* belong to it as do other soldiers in the backgrounds of the *Disasters*. So does Judith, a disturbing and massive Nemesis, all the singers in the *Pilgrimage to San Isidro*, its figure on the left – a woman pitcher-carrier without a pitcher – its fanciful hills, and especially the mass of its principal group, the mass which is separated from the

GOYA: *Mass for New-born Children*. Agen, Museum

162

GOYA: *The Last Communion of Saint Joseph of Calasanz*. Bayonne, Musée Bonnat

bay-shaped area that comes next to it by a deep cleft of light. This art, glimpsed in the *Mass for New-born Children*, reaches its culmination not in the *Milkmaid of Bordeaux* but in the *Last Communion of St. Joseph of Calasanz*. Can the art which will not lend itself to a glorified reality be anything but colour or architecture, or both at once? Goya now foreshadowed Manet, Daumier, and one of the aspects of Cézanne. For the latter to be born it would only be necessary – only – that art should be emptied of the metaphysical passion that played havoc with Goya, that it should itself become its only subject matter. In some of Goya's later portraits and in some of his later canvases it is tending that way. This man, whose fancy was his second life, and perhaps his first, was freeing painting from fancy. He was giving it (not with an involuntary spasm like a dying Hals, but persistently) the right to look upon actuality simply as raw material, not for the production of the kind of glorified universe the poets were trying to make, but to be turned into the specific universe that musicians know.

GOYA: '*For having lost his legs.*' Drawing. Madrid, Prado

'BETTER IDEAS THAN BEFORE...'

THE providential discovery of lithography (his weakened eyes no longer allowed him to etch) transformed his drawing. It had always been open to experiment but also it was too much the preparation for and the result of his engraving not to be affected by the radical changes in the latter. His patches of colour become more blurred, his accents less sharp. As much as ever he shuns Italian over-refinement, now neo-classical, but his style is hesitant before the stone, as was that of all the early lithographers.

Between his idea (or his model) and his pencil drawing there seems to be interposed a sepia from an earlier period, a sepia of which the drawing would be a

GOYA: *Mid-Lent*. Drawing. Formerly Madrid, collection A. de Beruete

Goya: *The Giant*. Etching

166

GOYA: *Saturn*. Madrid, Prado

faltering copy. His etchings had been simply engravings – his compositions and portraits are only paintings; but his drawings are based on a line which is unsteady and slightly crushed, and often of a lightness in colour similar to that of the engravings in which he had employed the technique of Tiepolo. He seems to be going back to his youth; as indeed he was, until the day when he discovered that the basis of lithography is not only black but white as well.

He had made that discovery once before in etching. At Bordeaux, where he could not take his painted monsters, he drew them again, but in his faltering drawing they also grew old . . . Yet once again, as at San Fernando, as with the darkness of the *Caprichos*, he hit upon it. By first spreading all over the stone a grey from which he would tear the patches of white with a scraper, he recaptured the black, the basis, the line so passionately authoritative – the accent of his colour. He stood the stone like a canvas on his easel. He gave up sharpening his pencils but used them like brushes. He strove for that effect of a composed unity which demands to be seen at a distance, the effect he had sought in his pictures but which no one for a

GOYA: *Bullfight*. New York, Metropolitan Museum

169

GOYA: '*The crowd, with lances, etc.*' Etching. (Tauromaquia 12)

long time to come would demand from lithography. And he ended by using the magnifying glass, not because of care for detail, which he avoided – but because his eyes were going . . .

As to the faltering hand of the drawings executed with a sharpened pencil, that becomes the old majestic scrawl. Not to produce monsters now, but to satisfy the other abiding passion of his life, the one he had known before the phantoms and against which they had not prevailed; even beneath the cry of anguish he had heard the muffled gong of blood. Here once again is the echo of the stilled clamour of war, the echo of the age-old voice of the Spain he had left behind – the bull.

He had previously devoted forty plates to it and many pictures. The *Tauromachia* was a wonderful collection. In spite of an apparent repetition where genius seemed to be wearing thin, each one of the compositions, with the exception of a few documentary plates (and even in them his hall-mark is not absent), had found again the grand manner. In every corrida there is the mixture of a spectacle from the circus (with its element of danger, but acrobats also are killed sometimes) and a communion in blood. Goya went from spectacle to communion, from the *aficionado's* pleasure to the celebration of a sacrifice. His other-worldly black was as much a part of his dealings with death as it had been of his witchcraft. And the bull, what-

GOYA: *Death of the Alcalde de Torrejon.* Etching. (Tauromaquia 24)

ever the subject of the engravings may have been, was always the bull. Harassed by dogs, picadors, and banderilleros, it never lost that pent-up immobility that Goya gave it so forcibly as it confronted the lances, the immobility that was to hurl itself into slaughter – on the scarcely lowered horns eviscerated horses or dead men would writhe in the succeeding plates. In the art of *Francisco de los Torros* what part had not been played by the combination of death, sport, and the dark side of the world! Certainly the corrida, its costumes, and its sacrifice were in his eyes a blood-stained carnival. From so many forgotten accidents and exploits there remained, when the album was closed, the silhouette, heroic in its animal fashion, that so often was to be seen against the sky above the ridges of Aragon, just as in times past the Minotaur had arisen before the slopes of the headlands of Crete.

Yet even the bulls now lose the muscular bronze sheen that etching gave them. Goya searched gropingly for the sparkle that his painting would find. For he still went on painting in that poignant light in which the approach of death brings together Titian, Hals, Rembrandt, and Michelangelo, old men weary of life but not of painting, turned away at last from mankind and painting only for themselves. Painters know old age but their painting does not . . . He worked at his last portraits, at the *Nun,* and the *Monk.* His haunted loneliness, a loneliness haunted now by the eternal as well, had joined the deafness he shared with Beethoven. But his drawings

171

GOYA: *The great Corrida.* Paris, Arthur Sachs collection

GOYA: *Bullfight*. Madrid, Academy of San Fernando

GOYA: *The Milkmaid of Bordeaux*. Madrid, Prado

were exhausted. He would have to change their style and find, in gouache no doubt, the equivalent of the whiteness of the scraped stone. He passed through Paris, saw – and disregarded – the *Massacres of Scio*. He drew the man-skeleton, the charmer of lizards and snakes, and the idiot; then, again, some flying dogs and a few laggard demons. Spain herself was remote from him, the Spain of which he knew that if

GOYA: *Utter Madness*. Drawing. Prado

GOYA: *The Sleeping Giant*. Drawing. Formerly Madrid, A. de Beruete collection

he had not painted her she would not be the same in the imagination of mankind . . . Yet she alone still knew him. A few artists alone realized that he was something besides a king of the picturesque. The reason is that only to Spaniards was the Spanish element in his work sometimes modern and sometimes nationalist but never exotic. In English and French eyes his mantillas, his monks and his tortures belonged to the theatre, almost to the imaginary. To Paris, a garrotted man was something unreal – a man guillotined would not have been. (He drew the guillotine, as it happens, but for himself alone, and without rediscovering his genius.) To

177

GOYA: *The Idiot*. Drawing. Formerly Madrid, A de Beruete collection

London, the figure in the *Monk's Visit* was first and foremost a monk; to Madrid it was the age-old apparition come from the world of the dead to demand justice, the apparition whose noiseless immobility puts to silence all the stir of human life and even the far-off rumble of the sea. He thought of new *Caprichos;* he had 'some better ideas than before'. His flattened manner now shatters the formalism of the *Agony in the Garden*, the shell-like coverings of the priests in the *Last Communion of St. Joseph of Calasanz* and in the *Mass for New-born Children*. A succession of paintings from which no picture could come, a style which aims not at light but at a powdering of colours to which Monticelli would later try to find the answer like a feeble echo of sadness, this is what emerges from his faltering drawings. The bulls with crows for riders that passed across the sky, the bulls that fell from it in rain in one of the later *Disparates*, reappear, scarcely discernible, in the epic hallucination of the last *Corrida*. He scarcely saw any more the world he heard no more; he began to be unable to see even his sketches . . . The stout *Water Carrier* becomes the *Milkmaid of Bordeaux* – we see the tremulous hand of the later Titians.

Soon painters would forget at the cost of what anguish this man had ranged his solitary and hopeless art against the entire civilization into which he had been born. From those still dazzling embers they would retain only the advent of the individual, the metamorphosis of the world in pictures. And yet . . .

'In such a night as this, . . .' In such a night the aged exile, whose deafness sent him to the fairs and roundabouts so as to avoid the gossip parties that brought his companions together at the house of the Valencian chocolate maker, still tried to make audible once again that voice that was the most eager for the absolute and the most remote from it that art has ever known. Perhaps it was on such a night that as he drew, half blind, the *Sleeping Giant*, he remembered that out of the anguish that never ends, beyond the dark cries of demons possessed in their turn, he had plucked the other *Giant* whose anxious face dreams amid the stars . . .

And now modern painting begins.

GOYA: *Self-Portrait*. Bayonne, Musée Bonnat

LIST OF ILLUSTRATIONS

WORKS BY GOYA

COLOUR PLATES

WORKS BY OTHER ARTISTS

'*Don't leave one of them*'. Drawing. Madrid, Prado